Who's the
Girl in the
Fat Suit?

A. L. Elder

Eight Paws Publishing, LLC

For more information:
Eight Paws Publishing, LLC
P.O. Box 846
Lebanon, Oregon 97355
http://www.eightpawspublishing.com

Who's the Girl in the Fat Suit?
Copyright © 2014 by: A. L. Elder

This book is a work of fiction with a
sprinkling of non-fiction throughout.

Who's the Girl in the Fat Suit?

Eight Paws Publishing, LLC
P.O. Box 846
Lebanon, Oregon 97355

Cover art by Gwen Lindsey
https://www.facebook.com/gwen.lindsey
Edited/proofread by Frozen Ladybug
Edited by: Hyde 'N' Seek Editing
http://the-gal-in-the-blue-
mask.blogspot.com/p/hyde-n-seek-
editing_1694.html

ISBN-13: 978-0615984018
ISBN-10: 0615984010

Printed in the USA

First edition: May 2014

0 9 8 7 6 5 4 3 2 1

Dedication

This book is dedicated to every woman who has ever stood in front of a full-length mirror and asked, "Really?"

Seriously, I'm normal!

I began writing this book with the goal that it would be hilariously witty. Somewhere between drafts, I found that I was a little narcissistic about my weight. I thought about changing the stories to make them more mainstream relatable. I gave it a lot of thought and decided there had to be other women out there who were like me. Maybe not in all aspects of this book, but I hoped similarities would pop up as they were reading through the chapters. That and I have to be honest and true to myself.

"Perhaps you shouldn't publish this one," a close friend told me after she read a few chapters. "It just makes me feel bad for you."

"Isn't there something about you that you wish you could change?" I asked.

"Sure, but I wouldn't want the whole world to know about it."

That's the kicker isn't it? We all walk through our day with a smile plastered on our faces, because we want the whole world to believe that we are happy.

Well, we all have bad days! We have those days when we wake up with a giant zit on our forehead. In a panic, we search the junk drawers for tweezers, because honestly, they are never where they should be. Anyway, we come across a pair of scissors and have an even better idea! Cover the blemish with bangs!

After spending not nearly enough time parting off a section of what looks like it should be bangs, we twist the hair and cut it off without thinking, or caring about the consequences of having to grow them out eventually.

Then, because we are not professionally trained in cutting said bangs, we end up with crooked, uneven locks that are far too short! Grumbling, we try in vain to curl the hair, and end up burning our foreheads with the curling iron. After all of that, someone makes a comment that we look nice with bangs!

Sigh.

We also have great days when our hair and makeup magically align to model perfection. We even take a little more time on our hair...curling small sections at a time. We walk into the office with a strut, until someone says:

"You look really tired today!"

Seriously? Dang, I was thinking everything looked pretty darn great today.

Yes, yes...it's the nature of the beast.

So, bottom line I suppose is this: I have issues with my body image. I wish I could wake up tomorrow morning and be the size I was ten years ago. Shoot, I would be thrilled to be the size I was five years ago!

I have negative inner monologue.

I don't find exercising to be enjoyable.

I like to eat fast food.

I love sugar and coffee.

I avoid mirrors.

I joke about my weight to take away from my insecurities.

I am what I consider a normal, over-weight woman.

I must caution you, though.

This isn't a diet book.

This isn't a how-to lose weight book.

This isn't a book that promises to improve your self-esteem.

I have learned there is not a one-size-fits-all program. You and I, while we may have similarities, we are different. We are motivated by different things and have different triggers to food. I simply want to share my story with you. We already have one thing in common, right?

Alright then, now that we have that out of the way, let's take a little journey. Together.

Table of Contents

What you see isn't always what you get.

Reality

Here's the thing...I have been friends with women of many sizes and shapes over the years. Some have been sickly thin, while others were morbidly obese. One thing they all have in common is a false reality of their own bodies.

We are hardest on ourselves.

We look in the mirror and wish for something we were not born with, or wish for something less than what we have. My skinny friends see themselves as slightly overweight. They make comments about losing five or ten pounds. My larger friends? Well, they see what I see. They see a skinny girl trapped inside a Fat Suit, even if they haven't been skinny in decades. I honestly do not believe that there is a woman out there who is completely satisfied and content with everything about themselves.

In this day-and-age, with plastic surgery and fake *everything*, it is easy to alter ourselves into something closer to what we perceive as beautiful. I am a size twelve-ish (depending on the day) and I am five-feet-seven inches tall...I am overweight.

I did an online search, because everything you read on the Internet is true, and found that the average size woman in America is 14. So, according to the Internet, I am below average, even if it is just barely. I suppose this is one time where being below average is a good thing.

Truthfully, though, I am one Peanut Buster Parfait away from average. Keeping this in mind, I shouldn't be so hard on myself, right? Easier said than done when you look at the way media spends billions of dollars to portray something quite different.

I say that carefully, though. There are several women in Hollywood who, according to the tabloids, are too thin.

Then there are others who shouldn't wear a bikini. There are others that claim to be wearing a bikini, but the tiny straps seem to disappear between the skin folds.

Somewhere in between those extremes is *perfect.*

Movie stars that the tabloids say are too thin look great on the big screen. For example, Angelina looked amazing in the tomb movies but was criticized for being too thin.

I heard that the camera adds ten pounds. Well, after attempting to upload a homemade video onto the Internet, I can tell you that the camera also adds a chin! (Okay, two chins. But really...who's counting?)

We have all witnessed the horrific effects

of too much fake when it comes to Hollywood. Actors and actresses with tight, alien-like features caused from too much plastic surgery. It is like a drug...or potato chips. One is never enough.

So, that brings me back to my first revelation, which is: We all wish we had something that we weren't born with. I laugh as I tell people that I was too busy chatting when the good "features" were being handed out. I imagine there to be multiple lines where we chose our best and worst features before we were born and we each chose which lines to stand in.

"The Gene Pool Livery," where you got to choose from your parents' best and worst genes.

I chose the shortest lines in an effort to save time. Everyone knows I lack patience! So, I picked, rather precariously, big green eyes, dishwater blonde hair, cankles after 30, large nose and undefined cheek bones. Oh, I also stood in the really short line that, to my surprise (and dismay), ended at the "gain weight everywhere" booth.

Seriously! I have earrings from high school that don't fit anymore because even my earlobes have gained weight!

Hair color, contact lenses, makeup, compression underwear, girdles, 4" heels, and acrylic—we have the power to recreate ourselves into the image we see in our own minds.

Are you ready for this?

We are about to embark on a little journey down the funny, dusty and sometimes dark roads of my transformation from a size four, a size twelve-*ish*. I will share with you how I have tried to change my self-image and how it blew up like a bad bag of frozen veggies in the microwave. In the end, I did defeat the Fat Suit and many of my personal demons. It was a very long and emotional journey.

I have deleted more than my fair share of ugly photos of myself.

Candid photos

I am always amazed by my own reflection. It is such a moment of reality when I catch a glimpse of what I actually look like. I mean, I have an image in my head and, well, it is completely delusional. I still see myself as a thin person with long legs and a flat stomach. The mirror, however, reveals every flaw I have tried in vain to disguise whether with makeup or false lashes. The mirror does not lie. It's not just mirrors, though. No, it's windows, photographs and videos too!

The worst, I think, are those candid shots that everyone thinks make great photos.

Really?

The last thing I want to see is myself as I

really am. Give me a stinking second to suck in my stomach and straighten my shoulders, for Pete's sake! Give me another second to contort my neck so that my chin becomes a singular object, rather than three consecutive rolls!

The candid photo is not my friend. When I find them in a pile or on the computer, I get rid of them. I have single handedly destroyed countless photos, because I do not like the way I look in them. After all, who needs that kind of reality?

If I am posing for a selfie, I may take upwards of fifty photos. (My cell phone has a very large memory card.) More often than not, I delete the entire file of photos because, what I see is not what I want to advertise to the world. I'm not ugly by any means—it's not that. It's that what I see when I look at myself is far from picture perfect.

Okay, so there are women that you look at from far away who are simply breathtaking. Those are the women I point out to my husband, Wes. Then there are those women who look awesome from far away and get homelier as they approach. I point them out to Wes too. Then, there are those women who smile as you pass them. They aren't gorgeous, but they aren't homely. They smile, which makes them more approachable. That is me. I am a smiling, approachable, not-too-pretty, not-too-homely woman. You most likely would not point me out or even notice me in a crowd. If you did happen to notice me you would probably feel pretty comfortable starting a conversation with me.

Now, if I am posing for a photo with another woman and they ask me if I think the photo is okay, I simply nod my head. If I am smiling (and my eyes are open) I am happy to let the photo go-forth-and-conquer. If I am posing for a group photo and, let's say, I didn't suck it in—well, that's all on me. I'm not going to insist the group reassemble on my account. It's the never-given-the-opportunity-to-put-my-best-face-forward, candid photos that I cannot allow to pass through my filter.

A professional pedicure done by an amateur is an oxymoron.

Acrylic toes

I warn you, before you even start this chapter, I do NOT recommend anyone trying what you are about to read.

Okay, now that we have that out of the way, let's begin.

It was almost Spring. Time for me to begin my annual preparations for sandal season. Usually, my toenails are short and cut unevenly, simply because nobody sees them inside my winter boots.

Usually, I begin by shaping the nails and allowing them to grow out naturally. It takes time and patience. While I had the time before the warm weather arrived, I did lack the patience to wait for my nails to grow naturally that particular year.

I decided I wanted beautiful French-tipped toenails and I wanted them now! The only way I was going to achieve the instant look was to either go to a salon or do it myself.

I chose the latter, unfortunately. After spending far too much money and time in the beauty supply store, I carried my treasures into our living room and arranged everything on the carpet. I had purchased an abundance of supplies from acrylic powder in pink and in white to an assortment of fake fingernail tips.

I stared intently at the tiny bottle of glue which promised to dry in five seconds, before placing it strategically on the floor. I had also purchased a brush to apply the acrylic, after asking the sales lady which she preferred.

I hastily opened the tray filled with different sized tips and remembered the sales woman telling me that I should roughen up my natural nail bed to ensure a good stick. She explained the glue would adhere best to a rough surface. She also said it would prevent lifting. (Something about natural oils, I think.)

So, I put the nail tray aside and began to file my toenails one by one. The process took a while, left a layer of fine dust on my clothes. I used some fingernail polish remover and a cotton ball to clean the excess dust from my feet.

I was finally ready to glue on the first nail.

I started with my big toe. I did a dry fit, just like the lady had recommended. When I was satisfied with the fit, I applied a little drop of glue to the back of the nail and pressed it into place. Viola! I had a toenail that was three inches long. I grabbed another nail tip, and another until all ten toes looked like some horrific foot version of a witch hand.

I was definitely going to have to cut them off. I looked around me, searching for the toe nail clippers only to realize I hadn't retrieved them from the bathroom before starting the adventure.

Oh well, I thought, I will just walk carefully across the room and find them.

The moment I stood up, I knew I had made a huge mistake. The three-inch fake nails dug into the carpet, like a cat at a scratching a post.

Pain! Pain!

I rocked back on my heals to relieve the pressure.

Better, oh so better.

My upper body was leaned forward to counter-balance my weight as I walked very carefully, on my heals, to the bathroom. I looked through the drawers and came up empty. Then I recalled that all of my polish and clippers were under the sink in a basket.

Why did I organize this stuff last week?

I go through these stages where I want our house to look like the most organized people reside within its walls. I take one room at a time and rearrange everything. I swear, if I had a label maker, life would be so much more exciting.

Wes loves it when I reorganize. His favorite so far was when I organized the kitchen. I took everything—and I do mean everything—out of the drawers, off the counter and out of the cupboards. I reorganized by placing the coffee cups in the cupboard above the coffee maker and placed our sharpest knives where the silverware once resided. Wes stabbed himself twice before remembering that the spoons were one drawer over.

So there I was, in the bathroom wondering how in the world I was going to crouch down and retrieve the basket under the sink without bayoneting the linoleum with my new toenails. Every possible solution I could conjure up wasn't pain-free, so I decided to just go for it.

I held my breath and slowly lowered myself toward the floor. I ended up losing my balance and landed flat on my backside with ten toenails securely attached.

Phew!

I carefully crossed my legs and scooted toward the cabinet door. The basket was way in the back. *Of course it was.* My knees were flush with the cabinet. I looked through the basket to make sure everything was there and, when I was satisfied, I untucked my left leg and scraped all five toenails across the bottom of the cabinet. It sounded like nails on a chalkboard, but felt like someone was removing my digits with a pair of pliers.

"Holy shnikey, oh dear rabbit, son-of-a-biscuit-eater!"

The pain was excruciating! Each toe was literally on fire with sensation. Three long, nearly clear, nails flew into the air like fireworks on the 4th of July, and small trickles of blood began quickly pooling on the floor. I had listened to the lady and filed my natural nails to ensure a good stick and she was right! Not only was I without three, three-inch fake nails, but I was short three natural toenails as well. The force ripped off my natural nails!

I thought I was going to pass out—right then and there—in our bathroom. What would Wes think when he got home and found me?

"I'm sorry son," the coroner would say, to my poor Wes, "It looks to me like cause of death was Toe Nail Vanity."

Oh, I am such a dork, I thought.

I turned my attention to the blood and the pulsating pain. Truthfully, the pain was subsiding. I think my body was going into shock.

Just then, I heard the dog bark.

Shoot, shoot, shoot! Crap, crap, crap! He's home early!

He would know I was up to something the moment he walked through the front door. I had made a mess of the living room floor with all of my nails, liquids, powders, adhesives and brushes.

It's not like this was the first time I had ever had a not-so-great idea. Fortunately, he came in through the back door and quickly found me sitting on the bathroom floor.

"What happened?" he asked, as he knelt down.

The pain was fading, but was quickly replaced by embarrassment.

"I tried to make my toenails long," I replied, staring down at my feet.

"I think you failed," he replied, shaking his head.

He wasn't even surprised. Like I said, this wasn't the first bad idea I had ever had.

"Where's the first aid kit?" he asked.

Hmm, where is the first aid kit? I wondered in my mind.

"I think I put it in the office," I finally replied.

Wes shook his head and retreated to the office. A few moments later he returned with the basics of first aid tucked in a little white flip-top plastic box. He bandaged me up, gave me some pain reliever, put me on the couch and propped my foot up with a pillow. I watched as he began cleaning up my mess.

"How much do your pedicures cost at the salon?" he asked.

"Um, I think they are $28.00, why?"

He shrugged and shook his head from side-to-side. "You do realize you could have had two pedicures for what you paid for your three-toe-removal, right?"

"Gee, thanks, Captain Obvious," I retorted, in my snarkiest voice.

That was the first and the last time I ever attempted to do my own toenails. I did, however take a crack at doing my own acrylic fingernails, though. Let's just say, Wes hid the power sander and I spent two hours in the nail salon soaking my fingers in acetone.

"Who did you say did your nails?" the red-haired nail technician asked.

"Um, she was, I mean, she's a friend," I lied.

"Is she going to beauty school?"

"No, not that I know of," I replied.

I saw a smirk appear on her lips and she didn't ask another question. I think she figured it out. When she was finished, she handed me her business card.

"April," she said, "Please, never, ever allow your 'friend' to touch your nails again."

"Got it," I said, and tucked her card in the back pocket of my jeans.

I never return an item I
purchase online.

The dressing room

I absolutely dread the dressing room. I order on-line in the security of my home office, and try the selections on once they arrive.

Why? Because, quite honestly, I am more apt to order the correct size on-line verses going into the store. I know it seems ridiculous, but the pressure to be thin and perfect is only intensified by the twenty-something sales clerks wearing the latest fashions in a size four just waiting to grab me a larger size. This, while I'm left staring at my—nearly naked—reflection in the drab mirror of a fluorescently lit dressing room. Now you tell me, what could be less flattering?

I am so delusional when it comes to my body image. So much so, that each time I walk into a retail store selling clothing, I am instantly drawn to the wrong racks. The racks labeled in the size I wore when I was twenty-something. I haven't been a size four since I met my husband some sixteen years ago.

So, here I was flipping through the slacks. Yes, I am old enough to call dress pants slacks. They are arranged from smallest to largest. The smaller sizes have cute pleats and buttons. The larger slacks have spandex and no fashion flare whatsoever.

I think the manufacturers do this stretchy addition for one reason and one reason alone: if they design a pair of pants that stretch to a larger size, women will buy one in each color. It's true, for me at least. If I try on a size twelve and the stretch is obvious, causing the pants to puddle at my feet or fall off my waist, I will purchase three pairs of the same pants in the smaller size. It is simple...I no longer wear a size twelve, I wear a size ten. Well, at least on the days I wear them. And it's not like I am running around announcing, *"I wear a size ten!"*

Seriously, that would be a bit much, even for me.

I compare it to getting a really great haircut. I ask the stylist to chop off three or four inches, and then ask them to thin out the heavy spots. It is one of my favorite weight loss moments! I love looking down at the pile of hair on the floor and thinking to myself, *shoot, I just lost a good five pounds!*

If only I could use those shears and clip a few inches off my hips. It would make shopping for clothes a lot more enjoyable.

Truly, what normally happens in the department store is this:

"Hi, I'm Jessica," a perky little sales clerk says, the second my feet cross the threshold of the store.

"Hi," I mumble and give a fake obligatory smile.

"Can I help you find anything today?"

Now, what I really want to say is: *Yes! Please help me find the zipper on this Fat Suit! I have looked everywhere...well, almost everywhere. Maybe it's just hidden too well for me to locate. Either that or crap, with my luck, it's probably broken.*

Instead I reply, "No, thank you. I am just looking."

The clerk gives me the once over. I know what she is thinking: *Oh, this poor, poor middle-aged woman. Doesn't she know that the plus-size store is just three doors down?* (The lovely, encouraging, inner monologue we were all blessed with.)

Seriously? She is probably thinking that she has to work all day while all of her friends are out doing something fun. But, noooo...in my head, all I think is, well, you know.

"Let me know if there is anything I can help you with." She smiles, and walks toward the cash register.

I don't like her! I know, I know...I don't even know her. Regardless, I don't like her. I detest how her perky personality matches her perky little body. That was me once!

If I could go back in time and warn the tiny me about the future I would! I would tell the skinny me—who thought at that time she was fat, *ugh*—to get on a treadmill as soon as she grew out of her size five jeans. I can't though, so instead, I choose a few items and Miss Perky assigns me to a dressing room.

In higher end retail stores, dressing rooms have great lighting and skinny mirrors. Designers know before construction that self-conscience women, like me, will be undressing and staring blankly at their reflection. Warm lighting adds a nice fresh glow and skinny mirrors increase sales, right? Well, therein lies the problem.

Why, you may ask? Well, while trying on clothes in a high-end dressing room, one is going to expect that the clothes to look just as great in front of a regular mirror at home with regular lighting. One would be terribly incorrect!

This is another reason I shop in the comfort of my own home. I have purchased so many shirts that looked amazing in the dressing room only to discover that the rest of my world is not surrounded by skinny mirrors or warm lighting. My own bathroom mirror, well you know, it reflects the truth—the cold hard truth of fat rolls and skin so pale in the winter time one can see veins. My skin resembles rice paper from January to December!

Not that online purchasing is foolproof. No, no it is anything but that. I ordered some shirts online and was excited to try on a red satin top in particular. It was gorgeous on my computer screen.

Why is it when you hold up a new shirt it always looks far too large? But, when you get it over your head it shrinks and becomes far too small? Am I the only one this has happens to?

I swear, I am between sizes and have been for the past ten years. A large is too huggy and an extra-large is just too sloppy. So which do I chose? Do I wear the size that hugs my fat rolls like cellophane wrap, or do I wear the sloppy one that advertises how truly insecure I really am?

Normally, I choose the sloppy, because the last thing I want to do is to stand all day long sucking in my stomach.

Here's another trick that hasn't worked out all that well for me. Shaping garments. We have all seen them advertised as miraculous products. They promise to hide back fat and smooth rolls so clothes fit better. They promise to give the impression that you have lost ten pounds just by using them. They're made for your upper body, lower body and there is even a full-body option.

I think this is a cruel joke. I say this because, if you have tried to put the purely spandex body corset on, you know that you drop ten pounds from the struggle alone. Not kidding here! I purchased a body smoothing top in nude with short sleeves. I took it home, laid it on the bathroom counter and stared at it, wondering if I had truly purchased the correct size. It looked tiny. In vain, I tried to pre-stretch the neck and arms to make them larger. Each time I would pull the material, it would simply return to its tiny original self.

I suppose that was the point when shaping your body, right? So, I put my arms through the holes and pushed my head through the neck only to realize that I was stuck. Seriously! The contraption rolled up and was stuck in my armpits. My arms were dangling at an awkward level, partially in the air and partially out to my sides. I call it my lazy scarecrow look.

I couldn't breathe! I started to panic and my pulse increased. Here is where the weight loss part of my story comes into play.

I tried to unroll the shirt, searching in vain for the waistband. I couldn't find it. It was rolled so tightly that I could not pull it back over my head either. I stood staring at myself in the mirror caught between crying and laughing, only to confirm my dilemma—I was stuck. Eventually, I was able to wrestle with the rolled up portion and tugged the material over my chest and belly. When I let go of the waist band, the shirt snapped into place like a rubber band.

"Ouch!"

Okay, so here's where the truth comes in. I turned so that my profile was present in the mirror. Low and behold, smoothed over fat rolls!

Small celebration dance.

I can only wear the body slimming gear for a few hours at a time before I feel physically ill. I think it's because my fat is compressed against my organs, and my body has a difficult time functioning under the pressure, (literally).

So, back to the red satin shirt. It was misleadingly gorgeous on the mannequin, but absolutely hideous on my body. It hangs in the spare room closet with fifty other shirts that didn't quite work out.

Ugh, work out.

That is what those hangers are waiting for: me to work out and wear those dang shirts.

If only I had whiskers!

Perception of space

"Oh, it's okay. I can squeeze through."

I cannot even begin to tell you how many times I have made this innocent statement only to find my body squished between an occupied chair and a wall. Like that isn't bad enough? After the person has scooted in their chair, I take a look at the space that I fit through.

Huh, a lot larger than I had anticipated.

In my mind, again, I am still tiny! It's almost like my weight gain happened while I was sleeping. Or, wait! Maybe, just maybe, I was abducted by aliens and...ooh! They impregnated me with one of their own, and the gestation period is fifteen years. Yes! Yes, I think that is what happened. Right? Yeh, not so much.

The last time this occurred—uh, the squeezing through small spaces, not the alien abduction—was during Thanksgiving dinner. The rule of the table is you sit furthest to the rear in order of getting your food. Well, I ended up at the head of the table at the far end, so I guess I was at the foot of the table. I finished up my plate and wanted some dessert. Who doesn't have dessert with Thanksgiving dinner?

I tried to sneak my way behind the six chairs without plastering myself against the wall. Failed miserably! I got to chair number four—the first with an adult occupant—and said the infamous line.

"Oh, it's okay. I can squeeze through."

Once again, I proved myself to be wrong.

Really? Do I really need dessert?

Hello! It's Thanksgiving people! Of course I got dessert. I had pumpkin pie with the whipped cream. Here's the thing, if you are going to do it...do it all the way, or don't do it at all.

That's my motto. Well, with dessert anyway.

The taller you are, the more you can weigh.

Platform shoes

"Are these for your daughter?"

Again?

The perky, twenty-something sales clerk asks the, what-she-perceives-to-be middle-aged woman a devastatingly ugly question.

Why is it, when you are twenty, you think anyone older than twenty-nine is middle-aged? I remember thinking the same thing when I was younger, and now? Well, I am pushing forty now, and I don't think forty is even close to middle-aged.

Anyway, there I was shopping in yet another store that catered to skinny little girls whose target ages ranged from not old enough to drive a car to *waaay* younger than me.

I get it.

I do.

But, there are times I get drawn into these stores like a moth to a bug zapper on a cool evening in the summertime. I can't help myself.

This was one of those days. It was inevitable! I was walking around the mall. (These were the days when the mall was the place to go. The only place where stores were always open and choices were endless. A time when vacant store fronts didn't exist for long, because everyone shopped at the mall. In my day, it was a Malltopia!)

The store that drew me in was aptly named for the age group it marketed. I was walking by, minding my own business, when a pair of camel-colored boots caught my eye. They were simply adorable. I immediately entered the store and tried them on.

Perfect fit. The boots themselves were suede and garnished with fuzzy cream-colored fur. They laced up the front and had a great platform heel. I stood and admired them for only a brief moment before placing the treasures back into the box.

I made my way to the register and smiled coyly at Perky Clerk. She pulled each boot from the box to confirm the sizes matched. After ringing them up and announcing the total, she asked the inevitable question.

"Are these for your daughter?"

No, Perky, these are not for my daughter! These are for ME!

"They are," I replied. *Seriously?* Why fight it, right?

"She will love them! My mom got me a pair last week for my birthday."

That's great, I thought as I handed her my card. I gave her a fake smile and tilted my head to the left to give her the impression that I was undeniably, impressed by her mother's taste in footwear.

I wore the boots. Oh, yes! I wore them so much that I finally wore a hole in the sole and had to toss them out. It was a sad, sad day. They were, by far, the best boots I have ever owned.

I graduated from regular shoes to platform shoes around the same time I graduated from a size nine to a size eleven. There are some risks one takes when wearing platform shoes.

I am not the most coordinated woman on the planet. In fact, I have had my fair share of occasions when gravity wins. I will share a few of my notable challenges.

There are two types of platform shoes.

Safe platform shoes have a flat bottom. The other type of platform shoes has a, well I am not sure how to describe them. It's still considered a platform, however near the toe it is beveled on the underside. They are extremely difficult to walk in, even for the most coordinated and balanced person. I have made the mistake of purchasing the beveled type. Again, please let me reiterate: I did not stand in the "balance line".

In high school/skinny years, I would model for the local mall. Twice each year they would put on a fashion show. If I remember correctly, one was for back-to-school and the other was for prom. Both were very big events where I grew up.

Anyway, I would walk the runway and strut my stuff. Comical, now that I think about it. Man, I thought I was all that and a bag of chips. (Stupid chips, that's half my problem now!) Of the four years modeling I never fell on stage. I think my coordination was best in high school.

Back to the platform shoes.

I was at a hair show—for work—when I was first introduced to the "other" platform shoes. The model room was filled with brightly-colored, thigh-high boots. Platform boots! I was intrigued, as was my boss.

"I get the pink ones," I squealed, racing toward the pile.

"I get the teal ones," she said, laughing and following close behind.

It took us a while to get our dress pants tucked into the boots and zipped clear up to our thighs. That was the easy part, as we soon found out. Trying to get upright from a seated position nearly caused both of us to wet our newly stuffed pants.

"Here," she said, holding her hands out toward me. "We have to help eachother up."

Pushing and pulling against each other we inched ourselves up until we finally found ourselves standing tall...very tall. I swear we were easily a foot taller.

About that time, our spouses walked by the doorway and took a second look. They stood paralyzed once they realized who and what they were seeing.

Models! Yes that is exactly what we looked like. Our dress pants were bunched up near our hips and resembled balloon pants.

Our expressions said it all.

We thought we looked amazing.

The boys pulled out their phones and started snapping photos as we girls did our best catwalk swagger, while attempting to cross the entire room.

Everything went well for me until I attempted to do the runway turn. You know the one? Where you pivot, jut your hip and send a wink into the crowd while gracefully twisting your body all in one violent motion?

Mid-wink, the beveled edge of the boot took me by surprise. My ankle twisted, my face contorted and I was heading face-first into the carpet.

Fortunately, Wes saw what was coming before I had time to scream. (Oh, that would have been memorable since the actual models were walking the real runway in the adjoining room!) Wes bolted toward me and caught me just before I hit the floor. My boss and her husband were laughing hysterically behind us. Did I learn my lesson? Nope!

A few years later, I purchased a pair of beveled platforms and wore them to work. Unfortunately, Wes was nowhere to be found and, needless to say, I ended up scraping my knees and hands on the concrete pad just outside the door of my office.

I sheepishly looked around the parking lot filled with my co-workers' cars and said a silent prayer that no one had seen my little display. I collected myself and sat down at my desk.

I could hear laughter from the conference room and was curious to see what was so funny. I gingerly made my way across the hall—my arms out as if I were walking a tightrope—that was when I realized that the entire office had seen my less-than-feminine fall! They were all still laughing minutes after it had happened.

"Nice of you to drop in for the staff meeting, Grace," my boss said.

Staff meeting? Crap! I had totally forgotten.

Someone pushed a box of tissue toward me and someone else pulled out a chair and offered a hand.

"Wouldn't want you to fall into your chair."

The room erupted once more in a fit of laughter.

That was the last time I put on a pair of beveled platform shoes. (Oh, there are still a few hanging around in my closet, though!)

Even my earlobes have gained weight!

So lucky

I am so lucky!

Hang in there with me while I try to explain this without sounding like I have lost my mind.

When I started to gain weight, I noticed it in my waist right off the bat.

Then, somewhere between sizes eight and ten, the weight began to equally distribute itself all over my body.

Seriously!

I even began to notice that my earlobes were getting thicker.

I went from a size seven shoe to a size eight...wide. That, in itself, was a moment of pure despair as I sat in the shoe store staring at all of the adorable shoes made for people with skinny feet.

Was I truly destined to a future filled with loafers and orthopedic shoes?

This brings me to another discovery about shoes I want to share.

It was late fall and I needed a pair of boots. Even with the inevitable weight gain, I still want to be fashionable, right?

I went to the shoe store and there was a pair of black knee-high boots in a window display that caught my eye right away. They weren't sparkled or full of flash. Usually, I am drawn to sparkles and flash like my dog is drawn to birds and clean underwear! (Okay, maybe it's only my dog that is drawn to underwear...clean or otherwise.)

These were just a simple pair of boots with a zipper that came to just below the knee. I thought they would be perfectly sexy, yet still professional enough to wear with a skirt.

I greedily grabbed the box, taking ownership immediately, and squeezed my right foot into the boot.

Now, here's the kicker! I pulled the faux-leather material and wrapped it around my calf.

Ready?

There was a sixty-foot gap between the two sides of the zipper! Okay, that might be a slight exaggeration, but there was absolutely no way I was going to get those suckers zipped up. I tried! I really gave it all my effort. I twisted my leg in every direction, and then flexed my calf muscles to see if I could get the three inches of exposed skin covered. I was determined to get the boot zipped.

I must have been struggling a little louder than I thought. I am sure the sales clerk thought

I was having a heart attack as she rounded the corner.

She looked down at the boot as her face scrunched up and her head tilted to the side.

"We have other styles to choose from," she said, staring at the gap.

I laughed. Not a funny *ha, ha* laugh. No, the awkward, *I've-been-caught-doing-something-I-shouldn't-be-doing* laugh.

Obviously, I left the store without the boots and with what was left of my dignity. It really didn't matter, though. I mean, in six month there would be a new sales clerk working there and I could go back. Unless, oh geeze, what if the story of the lady with the monster calves makes the monthly bulletin board? Okay, so that shoe store was now off limits! I would be so embarrassed to go back and hear the whispers and jokes.

"Hey, isn't that the lady that tried..."

Let's just move on before I finish my thoughts on that!

"When are you due?"

I'm not pregnant!

"When are you due?"

It is an innocent question. If I *were* pregnant I would welcome the small talk. But, I am not pregnant and never have been. It took some time, but I now recognize the warning signs. I know I'm about to hear the question, so I head them off be performing the "suck-in."

The suck-in? Oh, well, that would be the two-second warning when I sense a strange extended arm and the flattened palm of a total stranger aiming for [what they perceive] is a pregnant belly. The last time this happened I was standing—no trapped—in the checkout line at the grocery store. I had just finished piling all of my goods onto the belt and was rummaging through my purse for my wallet.

My purse is like a bottomless pit. It qualifies as its own magic trick. I fill it with "useful items" such as lip gloss, sunglasses, keys and my wallet. Then, the purse transports them to another dimension. It doesn't matter how large or small the purse is, everything eventually gets swallowed up and becomes difficult to find on-the-fly.

Huh, I thought, while rustling the bottom of the magical bag, *I forgot I had gum!*

Out of nowhere—okay, she was behind me in line—I felt a hand pressing slightly against my stomach. *Not again!* I quickly sucked in—but not quick enough—it was too late. Her hand had already made contact and constricting my bubble-wrapped stomach muscles was not going to deter her actions.

"When are you due?" she asked, as she smiled brightly.

Now, what does one say at a time like this? Do I smile back and tell her ten years ago? Do I take the high road and tell her that I only have a month left? I mean, come on already! And, even if I were pregnant why do people think it is okay to touch someone else's stomach?

I didn't want to hurt her feelings, but seriously! If I were pregnant, I would be advertising it with a proud-to-be-pregnant shirt. You know the ones I am talking about, right? The tight shirts that show every bit of the belly bump? Well, that's the problem isn't it? These days, there are women wearing tight shirts that have no business wearing tight shirts! I say this gingerly, of course, because these women are proud of how they look. Either that or their significant other isn't truthful when asked, "Does this outfit look okay?"

If Wes hesitates for even a second after I have asked that question, I stomp off to our bedroom and in a fit of frustration, flip through my closet looking for the XXL sweatshirt that screams my support for our local high school football team.

Just for the record, I do not wear tight shirts...ever! Not even to bed!

"Not soon enough," I replied. I shrugged my shoulders and turned back to the cashier.

I watched as he slid all of my choices across the scanner. Soda, chips, frozen packaged meals...sheesh, I should really eat better if people think I look pregnant!

If you are going to insist that I get on the scale, please allow me to keep my shoes on.

Let's get your weight

How about, let's not!

Every stinking time I go to the doctor, the nurse insists that I climb onto the old fashioned weighing scales.

"Would you like to remove your shoes?" she asks, while motioning toward the contraption. She presents the scale as if it were a game show gift.

"And your prize today is a fabulous blow to your already-fragile self-esteem," a velvety baritone announcer's voice echoed in my head as I stepped onto the scales.

My reply is always the same, "No thanks."

Leaving my shoes on during the process provides me with a warped excuse to subtract the weight of my shoes. Now, I have never been what you would call a math-whiz—in high school or in college—but I can easily subtract ten pounds. (That is my fallback amount.) It doesn't matter if I am wearing boots, flip flops or tennis shoes...they all weigh ten pounds!

About a year ago, I was having a lump in my breast checked out by the doctor, and my sweet husband went with me for moral support.

Sure enough, the nurse had the audacity to present the scales—in front of my husband! I didn't have enough going on in my head already? Now I had to reveal the one secret every wife keeps from her spouse—their actual weight!

It's not that I think Wes is oblivious to my weight gain. Not at all. He is very aware of my size. But the fact was I didn't want him to have a "number" stuck in his head.

I declined to be weighed.

Having no idea that I had the option to deny the scales, I took a chance...and fortunately the nurse didn't press the matter. Long story short, I had to have a mammogram and ultra-sound. Turned out, my breasts were full of cysts. The radiologist reassured us they were not cancerous. He explained a procedure for draining the liquid from the cyst should they become irritated or painful.

Great, I thought. *I am going to have lumpy, bumpy breasts for the rest of my life.*

Hey! It could be worse. Remember, Wes still had no idea what my "number" was, so all in all I was pretty pleased with the results.

"Yes, this is my natural hair color."

Natural hair color

I am asked what my natural hair color is all of the time. Well, let's see...

When I was a kid my hair was blonde. Then every summer it lightened to near platinum. The older I got, the darker my hair became, until it finally settled in as dishwater blonde. It's a remarkable color really. No real natural shine. Honestly? It looks a lot like the color of a mouse. Mousy-blonde. That just about sums it up.

I don't spend much time in the sun anymore, so my hair doesn't have a lot of natural highlighting.

I am blessed with thick hair, which is the perfect base for adding fake color...so I do!

I have been platinum blonde, jet black and every color in between. There was a time when I had red and green highlights for Christmas! (Not my best look—but, not my worst either.)

When my hair was long, changing color was limited to highlights or lowlights. I wavered between blonde with blonder and blonde with slightly-darker blonde. It wasn't until I cut my hair really short that I began to understand the meaning of *chameleon.*

One of the first color combinations that I tried was platinum blonde with black underneath. Which was awesome until some guy commented that I should wear safety orange if I ever decide to venture into the woods. He went on to comment that [from behind,] I looked just like the butt of a deer.

A deer? The butt of a deer?

That man had no idea.

The butt of a deer. *Good gravy!*

The comment stayed with me, and I finally changed my hair to jet black all over. No more butt-of-a-deer jokes.

I also got my eyebrow pierced.

"Why would such a beautiful girl poke holes in her face and want to look like a vampire?" one woman whispered to another, while trying not to look in my direction.

I might have taken offense, but she said I was beautiful! Or did she? I've seen vampire movies, and I would be happy to look as flawless as they do.

Sorry, I digress.

Anyway, like I said before...my hair has been every color imaginable. Some combinations have been successful and others, well, you get the picture.

About seven years ago I went too far and Wes put his foot down. I came home after a three-hour appointment at my favorite salon. My hairdresser was one of those stylists that had mastered the art of corrective color long before I walked through the door. She was fearless and had nerves of steel.

"You know, one of these days your hair is going to turn into spaghetti," she said.

"Well, hopefully not today, right?"

I wanted to go from jet black to platinum again. She didn't even blink an eye at my request. Instead, she mixed up a purple concoction and slathered it on my head. Twenty minutes passed and I was enjoying a hot scalp massage in her shampoo bowl.

"Hmm," I heard her say. "I need to break your base."

She left the towel in place—over my head, which should have been a clue—and headed for the backroom. I wasn't sure how she was going to "break my base", or even what that meant until I removed the towel and stared and the hideous reflection staring back at me.

Holy Martha May Who!

My hair was the color of a carrot. Not red or auburn. No, no it was the color of an actual carrot. A CARROT! Then I started looking a little closer. My roots were white, and then the hair turned a pale yellow and finally faded into carrot orange.

"Don't panic," she said.

"Okay?"

"We just need to get the orange out."

Another shot of lightener should do it."

"Alright," I said.

Twenty more minutes and I was once again in the shampoo bowl.

Voila!

Success!

I was platinum once more. I am telling you: see an experienced colorist when you want a drastic change. Do not try it at home.

I might add that all of the bleach had destroyed the ends of my hair so the damage had to be cut off. This would have been fine, except that my hair was only about four inches long before we started the lightening process. So, when we cut another inch off the ends...well, you can imagine Wes's surprise.

"You look like a boy," he said, as I walked through the front door.

"What?"

"April, you look like a boy. What happened to your hair?" he asked, as he walked closer.

"It's a haircut," I retorted.

His face scrunched up and a scowl began to appear.

"Oh, quit," I said, "It's just hair. It will grow back. In the meantime, I will just wear a little extra makeup so people don't think you're married to a boy."

Snarky?

Maybe, but I was right...it is just hair and it did finally grow back out.

These days, I stick to natural colors like black and blonde, red and black, you know...only the most believable unnatural colors.

I remember when shaving
only took a few minutes.

Hair removal

Somewhere in my

family tree there had to have been a Sasquatch!

I used to tweeze my eyebrows, but always had a few, alright, an entire colony that refused to disengage. My eyebrows extend all the way to my eyelashes and tweezing near your eyelids can be extremely painful.

It wasn't until I was in my early twenties that I started waxing my eyebrows. Well, I didn't actually do the waxing, I paid a professional. (Surprised?)

Good grief! Could you imagine the kind of trouble I could get into if I tried heating wax and applying it to any part of my body? (No, that is not my next chapter.)

I have never been brave enough to wax all of my body parts. I have friends who wax everything. (Yes, everything!) First of all, I can't imagine anyone other than my OBGYN getting to know me *that* well. Let alone getting *that* up close and personal for any length of time.

"Oh, it's really not all that bad, and your skin stays smooth for a long time," my friend, Amanda, told me after one-too-many pomegranate martinis.

Regardless, it is just not for me. If you are one of the many brave souls who go under the wax for smooth skin, I applaud you. I, for one, do not have a very high tolerance for that kind of pain, or what I perceive would be utter humiliation. I doubt waxing the nether region would do anything to improve my self-esteem. I have a very good feeling that it would have quite the opposite effect.

Co-workers can inspire greatness, right?

A few years ago, there was a group of five women in the lunchroom. I was one of the five.

"Do you shave your arms, April?"

"Um, I shave my armpits," I replied.

"No, I mean your actual arms."

I shook my head, no. I looked down at the thick blonde hair all brushed in the same direction across my forearm. I had never really paid attention to just how much hair I actually had growing on my arms.

When I was really little, my grandpa showed me a really cool trick. If you lick the palm of your hand and rub a tight circle on your arm, the hair will ball up into tight knots. If you have never tried it, go ahead. It hurts though! I am not going to sugarcoat that one. The most painful part was trying to unwrap all of those tiny hair knots without pulling them out altogether! Looking back, I'm not sure exactly what part of that game was fun.

"So, you guys all shave your arms?" I asked, staring across the table. Heads nodded in unison.

"Seriously?"

"You shave your legs, right?" one of the smooth-skinned women asked.

"Yes, I shave my legs!" I was slightly offended.

"Well, it's the same thing. Here, feel," she said, while extending her arm toward me.

Okay, so her arm felt really smooth. I couldn't help but wonder if I would feel a little more feminine if I shaved the blonde hair from my arms. It may not be a bad thing at all.

Before I go any further, please take a moment and look at the hair on your arms. Notice the way the hair grows or rather...how many directions the hair grows. Did you know that the skin around your elbow is as thin as the skin behind your knee? Well, take it from me, and the bandage company, this is a true fact.

I did it. I shaved my arms every single day for two weeks.

It felt awesome!

I was amazed at how much easier lotion was to apply and how quickly it soaked into my skin. Did it make me feel more feminine? Well, sort of I suppose. But, the time it took me to shave my arms took away time I should have spent shaving my legs. I had to make a choice and since no one, (other than Wes) saw my legs, my arms were as smooth as a baby's bottom while my legs would have made any manly man jealous.

I started shaving my legs when I was thirteen. I wanted to start much earlier, but my mom was insistent that thirteen was the magic age. Twelve and three hundred sixty four days old, and I was too young to shave. One day later, I'm old enough. Two hours after all of my guests left my thirteenth birthday party, my mom gave me a very small gift wrapped in Christmas paper.

I should explain. My birthday is the first week of January, just after Christmas. So, rather than scrounge for birthday paper, my family wrapped my birthday gifts in Christmas paper. It became kind of a family tradition.

That was, until I married Wes! He didn't like the idea one bit. He insisted that all of the birthday presents I received from him would be wrapped in appropriate birthday paper.

Back to the story. I unwrapped the Christmas paper and stared excitedly at the razors still enclosed in cellophane. Mom drew me a bath and carefully explained that I was only to shave to the moles just above my knees.

I have matching moles. They are actually two of the few things that haven't grown or disappeared over the past ten years. They are about two fingers above my knees on both legs. Those innocent moles were my "shave only to here" markings. I obeyed the rules until I moved out of my parents' house. Then, the rebel in me decided to shave way above my moles.

Oh! I was such a rebel!

These days, I have to shave my arms and legs on the weekends when I have all the time in the world to dedicate to the project. Anymore, it's really not that big of a deal since I haven't worn a pair of shorts in ten-plus years!

A few months ago, I was flat on my back at the hair salon getting ready to have my eyebrows waxed.

"Do you want me to wax your lip too?"

"My lip?" I asked.

I have hair on my lip?

I remember my Aunt using a cream-like bleach to lighten her barely-there moustache when I was a kid. I asked her once why she did that, and she told me it was because of the Italian blood my grandfather gave her when she was born. I thought it was weird that my grandpa gave my aunt blood when she was a baby. (Of course, I now know what she was talking about. He must have presented me with the same gift.)

"Is it really bad?" I asked, referring to my upper lip.

"If it were on my face, I would wax it," she replied. She started inspecting the rest of my face with the bright round contraption that magnified everything underneath it. "I would recommend your face too. Oh and your chin," she said, rubbing her fingers along my jowls. My hand instantly went to my cheek.

Now, I have always had a ton of fine blonde hair on my face. I am convinced this came from Italy too, or perhaps Sasquatch were from Italy. Either way, all I know was the older I got, the more hair everyone else seemed to discover on my body. But to wax it off? Really? I cringed.

"So, my brows, my lip, my chin and my cheeks?"

"Yes," she said, dipping the wooden stick into the pale pink wax.

Her reply left me feeling a little vulnerable and self-conscience.

I swear, if she would have asked if I needed my legs, arms and nether region waxed I probably would have told her to go for it. I was completely mortified to find out that my face needed to be de-haired. How could I have missed all of this when I spent an ample amount of time in front of the mirror applying make-up and fake lashes every single day!

My mind raced as she attentively removed the offensive hairs.

I have a mole, a real mole (not a Ted,) on my chin. It resides on the lower right-hand side of my face, just below my bottom lip and just above my jawline. I fully expect that one of these days it will sport one of those course, black, curly hairs that seem to appear out of nowhere.

I guess I had been so focused on that one area I hadn't noticed the crop of other hair growing at length all over my face.

"Holy cow," I squealed. "That packs a punch!" I squirmed, as she ripped the wax remover strip from my face.

Who knew the skin near your jaw bone could be so tender? Proving, once again, that I have a very low tolerance for pain.

I was in the pedicure chair a few years ago getting a professional paint job when, out of the blue, the lady asked me if I wanted my toes waxed.

Seriously? Do they do that? My toes? Good grief, what is this obsession everyone has about waxing every inch of hair on my body?

"Yes, that would be fine," I replied.

You don't know pain until you've had someone uproot the hair growing on your big toe! I swore aloud, right there in the pedicure chair. (I apologized of course, but the damage had been done.) Deep breathing and Jedi mind control enabled me to sit still as she painstakingly cultivated the other nine toes.

Never again! I thought, as I slid my flip-flops over my bright red toes. No, the polish was pink and white, but my toes, oh sheesh! Red as candied apples!

I kept that promise. That was the first...and last...time my toes were ever waxed. They have joined the rest of my body parts that are sheared. (Arms, armpits, legs, and toes.)

Wes made a discovery of hair on my lower back and decided I should know about it. Again, fine, blonde frog hair. Just a tiny little patch, no big deal, I will just add that to my list of things-to-be-shaved. So, now we have arms, armpits, legs, toes and lower back.

It reminds me of that song: Head, shoulders, knees and toes...knees and toes!

Some of the most beautiful women I know do not believe they are even average.

A tiny bag of self-esteem

It was Wednesday, and I was at work.

Now, I work with one of the most beautiful women in the world. Seriously, she could be a model. She has flawless skin, red hair and the fullest, most gorgeous eyelashes I have ever seen in person. Her eyelashes are like the models in the television commercials who advertise mascara.

She could easily be one of them. I, for one, would totally buy any brand of mascara that she was selling!

I was admiring her luscious eyelashes like a total stalker, and decided to ask her about them.

"What kind of mascara do you use?" I asked.

"Seriously?" Her voice had a high-pitched tone to it, like I had asked an unbelievable question.

"What?" I questioned, with my brows pursed together. Should I not have asked? Did I cross over into some forbidden zone?

"April," she whispered. "They are fake."

"Noooo," I said, taking a step closer to her and leaning toward her eyes. She smiled and nodded her head.

"You can't tell?"

"No, not at all," I replied.

The longer I examined them the more I realized no one could ever tell. Well, maybe someone with a magnifying glass, but who carries one of those around in their purse? I don't.

"Are they difficult to put on?" I asked, still befuddled.

"Not really," she replied, smiling. She quickly wrote down a few websites and instructed me to watch the tutorials before I attempted to apply them on my own. I was so impressed with the possibility of having long, luscious eyelashes I went straight from work to the drugstore.

I stood gawking at the display for a very long time pondering the many styles offered. They varied from natural looking to what I would consider "after-hours" lashes and everything in between.

Wow, those are awesome, I thought, as I reached for a pair of super long, thick lashes with black rhinestones attached.

I wasn't too sure they would be appropriate for work, but I just had to have them. I ended up selecting thirteen pairs of lashes and two tubes of adhesive.

Addison had cautioned that clear adhesive did not look good with black eyeliner. She recommended the black adhesive and I was following her suggestion. She was, for sure, the most educated woman I knew when it came to false lashes. Okay, she was the only person I knew who wore—or admitted to wearing—false lashes.

"Oh my," the cashier said, as I piled my new attempt at improved self-esteem on the counter. "Do you coach a dance team?"

"A dance team?" I questioned. She looked down at the multitude of eyelashes and back up at me.

"Are all of these for you?" The pitch in her voice told me that I may have gone a little overboard with my selections. I smiled as I felt the blood rush to my cheeks.

"Yes," I replied, shyly.

She shook her head in disapproval and my embarrassment quickly turned to curiosity. *Why should she care if I was purchasing a large number of fake eyelashes?*

"That will be $86.27," she said, staring at the tiny bag.

"Wow," I responded. "That seems like an awful lot of money for a little bit of self-esteem." I laughed. She didn't crack a smile.

Tough crowd, tough crowd, I thought, as I handed her the cash.

The first thing everyone should know about fake eyelashes is that they are very difficult to apply properly. There are rules and tricks which are not provided with the tiny tube of glue. I recommend—highly recommend—

applying false lashes for the first time on a day where you have nothing else to do—and nowhere to go. I would also recommend searching the Internet and watching a few how-to videos before even attempting.

Addison had given me a list of three videos to watch. Like a good girl, I (impatiently) watched the first one then raced to the bathroom to give it a whirl.

"Watch all three videos," Addison's voice echoed in my head.

I tuned out the voice and stared at the large selection now displayed across my bathroom counter.

Which ones? Which ones?

Do I really need to tell you which ones I chose?

Oh, alright…they were the fullest, longest, hooker-ish looking lashes of the lot. They looked like gothic butterfly wings—the pair with the black rhinestones!

The video instructions said to put a very fine line of adhesive on the base of the eyelash and wait about thirty seconds for the glue to get tacky. I waited a whopping ten seconds.

I lack patience, remember?

My first attempt was nothing less than a total failure. I placed the lashes too high and ended up with a double line of black eyeliner.

No big deal, I will just make the liner a little thicker today, I thought, as I pulled the lashes and set them back on the counter.

Reaching for my black liner pencil, I approached the mirror.

Dang it.

The glue was still wet, and when I opened my eye wide, the black adhesive left another black line in the crease of my eyelid.

Oh! Did I mention my first and second

attempts were done on a morning when I had to be somewhere? Oh, and not just anywhere, I had to go to work.

I smudged the line in the crease and applied some more shadow to kind of blend it in. It didn't look too horrible, so I continued by broadening the black line on my eyelids. I did the same on both eyes, knowing that I would probably make the same mistake again on the other eye.

I figured the glue on the lashes had probably dried in the meantime, so I applied another strip of black adhesive and waited the full thirty seconds. I placed the first lash as close to my natural lash line as I could and repeated the process with the second. I leaned toward the mirror only to discover that the lashes were making little contact with my eyelid.

I took the tip of my fingernail and pressed the lashes against my skin. Black glue oozed from every spot I touched.

Lovely, I thought. *Maybe I'm not cut out for fake lashes.*

In a moment of pure desperation, I grabbed my blow dryer, and through forced air, dried the goop completely.

It seemed like the right thing to do at the time.

The lashes looked fake. They looked nothing like Addison's and they were crooked. There was no going back, though. I applied mascara to my natural and the fake lashes, which I later found out was a huge no-no. I dried them again with the blow dryer and used the infamous eyelash curling contraption.

When I had asked Addison how she got the lashes to look natural, she explained that she crimped the natural and the fake lashes together.

"That way, your natural lashes combine seamlessly with the fake ones," she had said.

The crimper got too close to my eyelid and one tiny squeeze caused a trail of black tears to race down my face. Do you know what happens to fake lashes when you cry? They fall off.

Yes, my friends the eyelash on my right eye fell from my eye and landed in the bathroom sink.

It took a few days before I finally watched the other videos Addison had recommended. They were actually filled with tips and tricks to get perfect placement and how best to remove and store the eyelashes.

Lesson learned.

Next time I will watch all of the tutorials before trying to master the art of applying fake anything.

Seriously? We all know that promise will be broken! I am, if nothing else, consistently impatient.

"April? Are these your eyelashes?" I heard Wes call from the living room one Saturday morning.

I peered around the corner and saw him pointing to our dog. Curiosity got the better of me, and I walked into the room.

Sure enough! Our dog, Steve, found a pair of my sticky lashes and they had adhered themselves to his left flank.

"Yes," I replied, and pulled the lashes off of the dog.

"Is that one too?" Wes asked, pointing to the end table.

"Ugh. Yes," I replied, and stomped over to the table.

"How many of those things do you have?" he asked, pointing to the area rug. "They look like caterpillars."

"A lot," I retorted, starting to get a little annoyed. "Have you seen the mate to this one?" I asked, holding up a single strand of lashes.

Wes diligently searched with me, but we came up empty.

"You know," he said, "no one thinks they look real."

"What?"

"When you wear those things," he emphasized *those things* like they were diseased.

"When you wear them, people know they are fake. They make you look like a clown."

"A clown," I said, in a flat and utterly annoyed tone. "A clown? You think I look like a clown?" My head started bobbing and sarcasm filled my voice.

"No, not me, everyone else."

"Who? Who have you heard call me a clown?" Oh here it was. The moment where I was going to stand my ground!

"Sweetie," he cooed. "You don't need to wear fake eyelashes. Your eyelashes are perfectly fine just the way they are."

"Babe," I said, taking a deep breath. "I do have to wear them for the next nine months, so just deal with it."

"Nine months! Why?"

Because it takes nine months for a new eyelash to grow. Because I didn't watch the second or third videos. Because I should have watched them, and waited until I purchased the adhesive remover before applying said fake lashes. Because when I tore them off after wearing them all day, I may have removed all the natural lashes in the outer corners of each eye.

"Because that is how long it's going to take me to finish the Fat Suit book."

He gave me an odd look, and then replied, "You're writing a book about fake lashes?"

"Yeah, something like that," I said.

He grabbed one of his shoes and discovered the missing fake lashes. He reached in and pulled it out, barely hanging on to as if it were a spider.

"If you are going to wear these things, at least put them away so I don't have to find them on the dog or in my shoes."

"Deal," I said.

"Otherwise," he said, "If I find them, I am throwing them away."

I nodded my head in agreement. Strangest thing...I have lost a lot of false lashes over the past few weeks. I swear they attach themselves to everything. Either that, or Wes's caterpillar hunting skills are improving.

I get it. There are a lot of people who find the "F" word offensive.

Big bones

Who in the world came up with the term big bones?

Seriously, I get more offended when someone attributes my excess weight to being born with big bones than I do with the whole "Are you pregnant?" question.

Is there even such a thing? Big bones, I mean. Or, is that just another way of saying you're fat without actually using the "F" word? Here's how the conversation usually goes:

"Are you serious? You weigh 214 pounds? No way!"

"I do," I insist.

Why on Earth would I lie about such a thing?

My Driver's License is a lie. It indicates I weigh 189 pounds. Right! I haven't seen that number on the scale since, well, I am not sure. It's been a while—definitely before I got my new license!

More often than not, this is how the conversation goes:

"Yeh, I weigh right about 214 pounds," I say.

"I don't see it, I mean, 214 pounds?" (Whoever it is I am having said weight conversation with.)

Here's where the conversation turns.

"Yes, I really do! I really weigh that much."

"Well, you must have big bones."

NO! I scream in my head. **I DO NOT HAVE BIG BONES! MY BONES ARE SMALL...OR NORMAL...OR WHATEVER. I AM JUST FAT.**

I prefer the "F" word over someone saying my bones are big.

I had an experience at work where two very muscular men were showing my co-workers and me the workout equipment our employer had installed to encourage healthy living.

I do think it is admirable that my employer encourages such a lifestyle.

So, here I was, in a large room filled with people I know, two men who worked out constantly and equipment that is powered by motion instead of electricity. One of the men was talking about pull-ups and the importance of core strength. I, being the smart one, piped up and said, "Oh, my core is solid underneath all of the bubble wrap."

My co-workers rolled in laughter. Let's face it, my employer was hoping that everyone would take this gift seriously, but honestly? Who wants workout advice from two super-massive-muscular men? I had to break the tension.

So, from then on out, it was to be known that I had some massive muscle tone I had chosen to bubble wrap in an attempt to keep my muscles safe.

I haven't stepped foot in that room for over three years. The only time I did, I found myself walking on a treadmill to nowhere. What is the point? I could not convince myself that walking for twenty minutes was the best use of my time, especially when I didn't walk anywhere. No, no I would rather sit at my computer and read the latest celebrity gossip before work.

It doesn't bother me to tell people it's a fake.

Wedding ring(s)

My wedding ring is absolutely perfect, except for one thing.

It no longer fits.

For the life of me, I can't remember the last time I even tried to get it on. (My ring...that sounded bad!) Anyway, I recall the morning I took it off for the last time and placed it in my jewelry box filled with costume jewelry.

I am not one to insist on a piece of bling for every occasion. In fact, I prefer the cheap stuff to the real stuff any day. There's a reason for this, of course. Partly because there was a time period of ten years where I was gaining weight on a regular basis and found that a twenty-four inch necklace quickly became a choker. That and, honestly, there are so many other things I would rather purchase than a diamond.

Ooh, like a new fountain pen! Clad one of those babies in gold and I am all over it. Yes, I have a fetish with old fashioned fountain pens. Some women buy purses or jewelry...please don't judge me for my pens.

So, after that eventful day when I realized I could not squeeze my once loose wedding ring over my now sausage-shaped fingers, I decided I needed to find a replacement. Uh, ring. Replacement wedding ring, although if they made replacement fingers in a smaller size, I probably would have purchased those as well.

Do you have any idea how expensive a new wedding ring is? Ha! There was no way I was going to spend our hard-earned money on something I was pretty sure, eventually, I would grow out of again! Instead, I asked the very well-dressed salesman if he would size my ring finger.

"Are you getting married?" he asked, looking around the store for my lucky guy.

"I'm already married," I replied. "I just grew out of my wedding ring," I smiled curtly.

"Oh, well then! It's time for an upgrade!" He was far too excited. I mean, I just told him I got fat and grew out of my original ring, and he was ready to find a replacement and slide it on my sausage-shaped finger.

Really? Not so fast, Mr. Shady-Salesman-of-the-Month!

"Size six," he said, interrupting my thoughts.

"Thank you," I said. I turned and headed for the door. Yikes, that was kind of rude! I turned over my shoulder, trying to save grace and said, "I will tell my husband to ask for..."

"Gabriel," he replied.

"Of course. I will have my husband ask for you, Gabriel. Thank you for your assistance."

Why is it, when we are shopping in a high end store, we use proper mannerisms? It's not like I would have used my British accent in a dollar store. I don't know. Maybe it's just me.

Anyway, I went home and searched the ole Internet for fake diamond rings. Wow! Now there's a business opportunity I missed. Hundreds of thousands of images popped onto the screen as I slowly scrolled down. For the price of a movie and dinner I could get a ring that looked like that? Wow-za!

I saved three, the best three, and asked Wes for his opinion.

"I think they are all pretty," he said.

That's it. That was all he said. He walked out of the room and left me befuddled and staring at three gorgeous rings. How was I going to choose just one? Wait. Is there a rule that you can only have one?

Obviously not! I mean, I already had my original. What would be the harm in ordering all three?

I could hear my mother's voice in my head telling me not to be greedy and choose only one. I didn't listen! I ordered all three and waited with anticipation for the delivery truck to pull up to the front out our house.

Glorious! Fabulous! Strikingly beautiful. I said, in my mind, as I tried each one on. Of course I said the words in my glamorous low voice drawing out each syllable.

The rings were quite amazing. They were also quite huge. Not the rings themselves, no they fit perfectly. The diamond wannabees were far larger than they looked online. Oopsie!

So, when someone comments on gorgeous my wedding ring is, of course I tell them it is fake.

What?

It is huge!

Trust me, if you knew me in real life, you would never believe that I would approve of spending a ton of money on a ring. It is just a token to tell everyone that I am promised to the man of my dreams. Who cares if the ring is fake? My love for Wes is one-hundred percent real.

Exercise should be a dirty word.

Twenty minutes

I am a twenty minute project gal. I have a very short attention span when it comes to crafting, organizing or cleaning. Trust me, I am only good for about twenty minutes. So, I was sitting at the computer the other day and I had an epiphany! I have always heard that working out twenty minutes per day is all that is really needed to lose weight.

I can do that!

I can totally commit to twenty minutes.

I turned off the computer and went straight to the bedroom.

Maybe I can do a before and after photo in the back of the Fat Suit book. My mind raced.

I was finally feeling motivated to shrink the Fat Suit.

I have tried the whole exercise thing in the past and never stuck with it. I have the necessary workout items, I just rarely use them for that purpose. I found a pair of yoga pants in the bottom drawer of my dresser and put them on.

I scattered the bras in my dresser drawer around in search of my constrictive sports bra. Now, there is no reason to believe that I am going to do anything that would require such support. But, if one is going to dress the part, one must wear a sports bra, right?

Looking at the innocent item one may become entranced by its simplicity. That is, until you pull it over your head and it twists into a boa constrictor. I spent the next few minutes contorting my flabby torso and pulling the material out of my armpits. Believe it or not, after untangling the many rolls on the stupid bra, I realized I had put it on inside out.

Seriously? After all of that?

I won't lie. I was a little out of breath from the wrestling match. I pondered for a moment and wondered if it was as difficult for skinny people?

Hmmm.

No one was home and no one would see it under my massively large sweatshirt. And besides, I had made a commitment to work out and a silly inside out sports bra wasn't going to deter me.

I grabbed a pair of socks and started to feel excited.

I am going to work out! I am really going to take the first step in losing this silly Fat Suit, I thought, as I skipped to the closet.

Shoes...where are my tennis shoes? I looked all over the house. The bedroom, the living room, the shoe closet in the main entrance. Nothing!

Where are my shoes?

My excitement was quickly fading.

I finally located them in the spare bedroom. Obviously, *someone* had thrown them haphazardly into the corner.

Wonder who that could have been?

I laughed and walked into the living room with my hardly-ever-been-worn treasures.

I sat down on the couch and put the shoes on the carpet at my feet. I stared at the clock in shock. It had taken me eighteen minutes to get ready for my workout.

"Well, a two-minute workout isn't going to do me any good," I justified, aloud.

I did put my tennis shoes in the shoe closet, though. I wanted to be sure they would be easily accessible the next time I get inspired to workout.

Denial is best served in front of a fogged mirror.

Reflection

I like to take very hot showers for a number of reasons. Of course, a hot shower is way more relaxing than a frigid rush of pelting ice water against my skin. But that's not the only reason I prefer it. I enjoy the fogged bathroom mirror as a side effect. With a mirror adjacent to the shower, I like stepping out to a fuzzy outline of what I actually look like.

Why?

Well, it's much easier to bear, (no pun intended) looking at a fuzzy blob rather than, well...you know.

It was a chilly October morning, and Wes had turned the furnace on in order to take the chill off the house. He had no idea how detrimental his efforts would be to my fragile ego. The furnace heated the bathroom, as I let the very hot rain beat down on my skin. I opened the shower curtain and immediately noticed the absence of mist.

There I stood staring straight into a non-fogged, clear as the sky in summer, reflection of myself. I froze. The reflection was completely foreign to me. Water was dripping from my hair as I stood shell-shocked—mesmerized by the large lady looking back at me.

"What the…" I whispered. *When did this happen? When did I go from a fit, trim size four t-t-t-to this?*

My reflection looked as confused as I did. As if the frame wasn't bad enough, I focused in on my face and realized I hadn't scrubbed all of the black eyeliner away. Upon further scanning, I realized my once prominent collar bones had disappeared. I ran my hand along the place where they once rested, adding shape to my upper torso, and found them hidden under the layer of squishy skin. I raised both of my arms over my head and smiled. What else could I do? It was too early in the morning to cry.

Well, that's where my breasts used to be, I thought.

My smile quickly faded to a scowl as my eyes surveyed the remaining damage.

Ugh.

My stomach was large and had somehow lost all of its shape, or maybe I should say it gained shape in the wrong direction. The skin, okay, the fat was too much to comprehend. Using both hands, I pulled the excess skin and fat toward my chest. It actually smoothed out significantly, and I began to see what resembled the skinny me peeking out through the Fat Suit.

Without thinking, I turned 45 degrees in

the shower…

Holy crap! I have back boobs!

I had heard of these, but never thought I would be sporting a pair in my lifetime. In horror, I released the abundance of belly fat and watched as it sprang back to where it had become most comfortable.

Back fat. I have…oh my gosh!

Yes, there was more! I stared at my round rump in shame. My gluteus was definitely maximus!

I have always had a well-rounded backside, even when I was skinny. But now? Holy mother of pearl, the thing was gi-stinking-normous! I am not sure how to explain it, except to say that it looked like a bad-cartoon version of a bumblebee. Ever heard of junk in the trunk? Well, I was staring at so much junk that I wondered how the trunk ever latched closed! I giggled. Even with this somewhat humorous undertone, I was still shocked by the figure (or lack of figure) staring back at me.

I like my world better! That imaginary world of, "Yup, I'm feeling good about myself today."

Honestly, most of my days are positive and I don't really think about those extra pounds clinging to my frame. In fact, if you look at the cover of this book, that is "my perception" of reality. In most aspects of my life I am a thin, confident and beautiful woman.

I was going to have to talk to Wes about turning the furnace on, only after I had taken a shower. This nonsense of seeing my naked body in a mirror was just too much!

Never, ever ask a question if you are not 100% sure of the answer.

The moment of truth

Motivation to exercise does
not come often for me. In fact, the last time I
remember wanting to exercise was after Wes and
I got into a discussion about my weight. Anger
and frustration have always been great
motivators for me. The problem with that is I am
normally a very positive person.

Anyway, Wes and I were sitting in our
living room watching a documentary on eating
disorders. The last story aired was about a man
who had a feeding fetish. His wife weighed in at
over 400 hundred pounds and the story revealed

that her husband fed her and encouraged her to gain even more weight.

During the commercial break, I turned to Wes and asked if he thought the story was interesting.

He grunted.

"Do you find me less attractive since I have gained weight?" I asked.

The little voice inside my head screamed, **"WHAT ARE YOU THINKING?"**

I stared at Wes, whose eyes were glued to the television. He was clearly intrigued with the golden retriever racing through the hallway of a strange house looking for bacon.

I should have left it alone. I should have assumed he had not heard the question, but I didn't. Rather than listening to the loud little voice inside my head, rather than thinking of the consequences of my question, I asked him again.

"Wes," I repeated. His eyes met mine. "Do you find me less attractive now, than you did when I was skinny?"

Silence filled the room like a thick fog.

A pause is a moment.

A pause is easily recognized.

Even as a small child I understood a pause in conversations. Too many seconds passed before I realized he wasn't pausing the conversation, he was trying desperately to avoid it all together.

Someone get the man a candy bar to chew on!

There were only a few reasons why Wes avoided a conversation with me in the past. Like, when I would ask him if a pair of jeans made my butt look big and he would not answer directly. Instead, he would say something to the effect that I looked nice.

Wes knows my insecurities like he knows

the color of my eyes. There was a time when he carried a small card in his wallet that had all of my clothing sizes on it. The most recent list was updated when I was a size nine. Yeh, that was quite a few years ago.

Why did Wes have the list? Well, it was actually something he had asked me to do one year before Christmas. He wanted to be sure to buy the right sizes. Writing the list was once an easy task. Tops: small, pants: five, bras: 32B, undies: medium. Once the sizes grew to large, nine, 36C...I just stopped torturing myself and refused to update his list.

Honestly, though, Wes has always had a good sense of what I should wear even with my ever growing body. Now, for Christmas, I ask for socks. That is the only size I don't mind sharing.

"Honestly?" Wes asked.

"Well," this time it was me who paused.

Do I really want an honest answer?

I nodded my head.

"A little," he sighed.

A little? What does that mean? Okay, I asked for it right? I mean, he gave me an out. I knew he wasn't interested in the goofy dog on the commercial. I knew what his answer was going to be before he had spoken it aloud. Well, I thought his answer was going to be way worse since I didn't marry a man with a feeding fetish.

So why, knowing what I knew, were my eyes filling quickly with saline? Why was a knot forming in my stomach and making its way to the base of my throat? Why was I still sitting on the couch next to Wes?

"It's not what you're thinking," he finally said. He grabbed my hand and stared as the tears began racing down my cheeks. "You're different now. I mean," he paused. He shook his head and lowered his eyes to my trembling fingers. I could feel my lip quivering. The knot in my throat was so large that it didn't allow a single word to pass.

Of course I am different now, I thought. *I went from normal to average. I am a water buffalo!*

I snorted, in an attempt to take a deep breath.

"April, I fell in love with an independent, vivacious character that could care less what the world thought of her." Another pause, five more tears.

"Ugh, why do I always walk right into these conversations with you?"

It wasn't a question although, he did end the sentence as it was. I couldn't answer. His words were recycling through my mind like a hamster running infinite circles on a wheel to nowhere.

"And now?" I choked the words out. I pulled my knees to my chest and grasped them with my arms trying desperately to make myself look smaller. It didn't work. Instead, I felt my large belly inhibit my knees from making contact with my chest. I didn't feel smaller. I felt huge. I wanted to disappear. I wanted the couch to open up and transport me to another dimension.

"Now? You are less sure of yourself and the way you look. You think that you are this unattractive, overweight person and it shows. It rubs off on other people."

What follows a stream of tears? Right, a runny nose and snort sobbing. Wait for it...ah yes, there it is. I began to puddle in front of my husband of almost seventeen years. Wes: a man of whom I had spent nearly half of my life with.

I puddled in my own self-pity and snot. My shoulders fell forward as Wes left the room. I knew for sure he was packing his things and leaving me. I am not sure why I thought this. He had never done anything like that before. I mean, we had experienced a lot together in the past. From losing our jobs together to purchasing our very first home...we had always been together. He had been my best friend, holding my hand and leading when necessary. Now, he was walking away.

"Here," he said, handing me a wad of tissue. "Honey, you need to either get to point where you are comfortable inside your own skin, or do something about the weight."

He said it like he was ordering a salad and steak. Although, Wes doesn't really like steak. That's me. So, I guess it was like he was ordering a salad and chicken. Yeh—that's more like something he would order.

His tone was nonchalant, like he simply had to state the words and my demeanor, my tears and my saline supply would cease.

I didn't respond to his words, but I did take the tissues. One by one, I saturated them with...well, you know what tissues are for. There's no need to get all graphic here.

That second after the storm when your body is exhausted, the water works subsided and you felt refreshed. But, I didn't feel that sort of relief. Instead, I felt embarrassed about my Fat Suit all over again. I knew that I could lose the weight. I knew that it would take work. I knew that Wes was right about my awkwardness and inability to feel comfortable in my own skin. I knew all of this, so why was I still bawling like a child who had fallen from the monkey bars?

"April, you are still the same woman I fell in love with," he whispered. "You are still the most beautiful woman I know. I just wish you would recognize that in yourself."

He was right, you know? I had changed. I

had become this fake representation of what I thought was beautiful. I had been trying to change my reflection when what I really needed to focus on was my perception.

"Hey now," he said, running his hand up and down my back. "Remember the time we went to the amusement park and realized there was a water park too?"

I nodded into my knees.

"What did we decide to do?"

I looked up and smiled. It felt good to smile. I rubbed the tissue over my eye and looked down at the fake eyelash now attached to the tissue.

"Do you remember?" he asked.

I do. I do remember, I thought to myself.

It was the middle of summer and we decided to spend the day riding roller coasters. When we arrived at the park, the ticket taker asked if we wanted a pass to the water park as well. This was during my skinny days, so why not, right? We dashed over the water park and changed into our swim wear. Wes had worn his board shorts, so it was easy for him. Me? Well, I will tell you, Victoria shared all of her secrets that day. I had worn my red flannel bra and pantie set that morning and honestly it covered more than a normal bikini for sure. As I walked out the women's dressing room, Wes was waiting and anxious to get in one of the lines.

"Ha!" he laughed. "You look hot in your underwear."

"Shhh," I poked him in the side. "Don't be announcing that! They would probably kick us out of the park if they knew."

"Really?" Wes asked. "Well, they would have to kick her out too," he said, pointing over my shoulder.

I turned around slowly, as not to look too

obvious, and quickly recognized my make-shift bathing suit on another patron at the park. She was larger than me. *In fact, she was the size I am now.* I remembered thinking that she must have somehow come to the same conclusion about bikini coverage as I had.

"April," Wes said, quietly bringing me back to the couch. "What did you say about that woman dressed in the same swim suit?"

I sighed, a deep, healing breath. "I said, 'she must have a really solid self-esteem.'"

I had said this because she was, in my opinion at that time, too large to be sporting a bra and pantie bikini. I sat and pondered my own impression of that woman and compared her to my newly found Fat Suit.

I was not comfortable in my own skin. I would die before I would wear a bikini. Truth be told, I would wish for death before putting on a one piece swim suit with a full length cover up. I didn't want to advertise my weight, my insecurities or my inability to commit to changing my outward appearance. The tears began to flow once more.

Wes lifted my chin and stared at me. Not an uncomfortable stare, no, he stared through me.

I was mesmerized by his gaze. *What is he doing? What is he thinking?*

"There she is," he finally said. "April, I fell in love with you. Just you! I fell in love with the girl who could take any moment and make it funny. The girl who could care less what other people thought of her cuffed jeans and mismatched socks. I fell in love with your imperfections, your love of Italian food and your strong sense of self. You used to be a tyrant. A force to be reckoned with. Now," he paused, and took a deep breath. "Now, you are so uncomfortable in your own skin and it shows. I'm not trying to be cruel, but you need to decide if you can live with yourself, and be happy at the weight you are."

I stared at him and said nothing. He was right, I had changed. I had become consumed by the Fat Suit. I avoided mirrors and became irritable when we had to go out of the house. Not because I didn't want to be with him, no, it was that I was ashamed of what I had let myself become over the years.

I never thought I would wake up one morning and be the size I am today. I never paid attention to my weight gain. I wasn't happy, but it was what I had to work with.

"I don't know," I replied.

"You don't know if you can be content with who you are?" he asked.

I shrugged, "This isn't me. This isn't the *me* that I want to be."

"Then, tell me what I can do to help you be the person you want to be."

The truth of the matter was: Wes couldn't help me. I had to help myself. I had to figure out a way to be happy in the Fat Suit, or decide to lose the weight and find happiness in a smaller me. I had to rediscover who it was that I wanted to be. Trust me, it wasn't easy. It wasn't pretty either, but I was determined.

I tried to love myself in the Fat Suit. I tried. But, in the end, I failed.

The darker side

If it weren't for my ability to laugh about my delusional reality of self, I am afraid I would never crawl out of my own bed each morning. Seriously! My weight gain didn't happen overnight. However, the realization that I am overweight seemed to hit me one morning as I stood in front of the mirror.

"Are you going to get up today?" Wes asked, as he walked into the bedroom.

"No, I thought I would just stay here until I lost seventy pounds," I replied, my tone thick with sarcasm.

"What's going on?" he asked. He plopped himself down on the bed.

"I am just tired of being fat. I am tired of thinking one thing and seeing another. I am tired of..." The water works started.

"So, your plan is to stay in bed for the rest of your life?"

I snorted, "You think it will take that long to lose this Fat Suit?"

Wes was rubbing my leg and, although I knew he was trying to provide comfort, his touch was just a reminder of what I had let myself become. My mind raced with possible solutions.

"Maybe I can find someone with mononucleosis and share a straw with them," I said.

"What?" Wes asked.

"You know, get mono. Then I wouldn't be able to get out of bed. I have heard people lose a lot of weight after being that sick."

He shook his head.

"No? Well, what if I could find like a tape worm pill?"

Wes snorted, "You would be willing to swallow a tape worm? Good grief, who are you and what have you done to my wife?"

"It's me," I said. "I just don't want to be like this anymore, Wes."

He adjusted his weight and I curled into a ball, a large ball, in his arms and cried with all of my might into his chest.

So now what?

Did I continue down the path of ignoring and joking when I catch a glimpse at my reflection? Or, did I decide that I am tired of torturing myself and get busy being healthier?

It's a toss-up, and I will be honest with you. While I want to be thin again, I am not sure I have the patience to do so. I mean, I gained weight everywhere and over a ten-year span. My false reality is to lose the weight overnight and somehow be the *me* that I have always known existed inside the Fat Suit.

More importantly, I am not really sure where to begin. You even mention you're thinking about losing weight and suddenly you are bombarded with information.

It's like when you buy a new car only to realize that there are fifty cars just like yours in town. Honestly, the cars have always been there. But you become more aware of the make and model, because you just spent an arm and a leg to finance yours.

That is what it was like for me when I decided to lose weight. Every third commercial was about a weight loss drug. Side effects include nausea, headaches, internal bleeding and for those individuals named, April, this drug has been known to cause death. Alright, so that last part is a little exaggerated.

Then there are the commercials for non-FDA approved drugs. No need to diet or exercise, the drug will dissolve the fat for only $69.99. And, they will even throw in a second bottle if you pay shipping and handling. Really?

How about the commercial for the food that is delivered to your door? Has anyone else noticed that they feature twenty-somethings having the time of their lives while riding a bicycle? To me, this screams false advertising. Are the advertisers marketing skinny, healthy twenty-somethings?

My favorites though, are the women who have lost 80 pounds and claim they are a size four. A size four? Um, I remember being a size four and those women are not even close. Maybe a size eight...tops, but a size four? It might be the wide screen television that we have that makes them look larger than a size four. All I know is when I finally made the decision to lose the excess weight, my thoughts and inner dialogue got all worked up and excited. That excitement only lasted about, yup, you guessed it, twenty minutes.

My pants started cutting off the circulation from my stomach to the rest of my body, and before I knew it I was purchasing a size sixteen. Well, so much for being below average. A sixteen! It's like I skipped fourteen and...oh Lord.

No one noticed, except me. I noticed! I couldn't believe that I had been denying my weight gain through an entire size! How does that even happen? My twelves were now in the second closet, and I was once again shopping online with frustrated vision.

I thought size twelves were full of spandex and blah...well, sixteens were no different. I wasn't entirely sure I really was a sixteen, so instead of committing, I ordered pants with elastic waistbands. The feeling of throwing in the towel, admitting defeat and returning to bed was all-consuming.

What was it going to take for me to really get motivated to find my own happiness? How much larger would I allow the Fat Suit to grow? What the hell was I doing?

I wasn't happy. I wasn't content in my own skin. I shuttered as I walked past a mirror or a row of windows. Yet, I was still partially delusional about my actual size. I was still a size four in my mind. I thought, in the end, I was going to have to really decide what I wanted. A false reality? Or the reality I could make by investing a lot of time and energy?

So, the weight loss journey begins.

Gastric bypass?

Okay, that was a little heavy, right? I mean, who lies in bed crying all depressed every so often? ALL OF US, right? Fortunately, though, we drag ourselves out of bed and pray once more for foggy mirrors.

Well, not this time! I decided that I was sick and tired of feeling like a water buffalo, and put my foot down.

Not in a literal sense, after all I had really no game plan to lose the weight that had so happily distributed itself all over my body. I just knew that something needed to be done.

So, where did I start? The Internet, of course. Ah, my friend and silent partner.

Hello Mr. Mouse, Mrs. Key Board and high definition screen. Let's see what we can conjure up this morning.

Wait! I am going to need another cup of coffee with a few more rounded tablespoons of sugar before I start this project.

Okay. Showtime! I searched for weight loss and the first thing that popped up was gastric bypass surgery.

Seriously? I have to have major surgery to lose this weight?

I haven't had anything major, as far as surgery, in my entire life. When I was five, I had to get stitches in my lower lip because of stubbornness.

I was in kindergarten and it was during recess. There was this contraption called the Witches Hat that I loved playing on. It had a metal pipe running up the center with chains that attached to a circular double bar. Kind of like a tepee shape or a witches hat. Huh. I suppose that is where it originally got its name.

There was an older boy in the middle turning the contraption too fast. Like a merry-go-round, but in the air. My feet were parallel in the air to my body. I told him if he didn't slow down, I was going to let go. Well, he didn't slow down and yes, I let go. My poor little kindergarten body slid across the asphalt like a ragdoll. Somewhere between two and three seconds, my bottom teeth penetrated my bottom lip. It was a bloody mess. I remember I was wearing my favorite white and burgundy dress that day. Red, white and burgundy after I finally reached the front office.

I remember the school nurse called my mother and told her that I had an accident. She told her that I had scraped my lip and my mom should come and pick me up from school.

Turned out, it was more than a little scrape. It required over one hundred stitches on the inside and outside of my mouth. This was the one and only time I have ever had anything that required medical attention. So, the idea of gastric bypass surgery was really out of the question.

I read the blip of information though. I mean, it's just information, right? Well, after reading, I discovered that I am not even qualified to have the surgery anyway. There is a minimum weight/body fat index requirement.

Well, isn't that nice.

I am too fat to be comfortable in my own skin, but would need to gain even more weight to qualify for the procedure. I mean, come on already!

I have discovered that I am a meat-eater!

Let's try a Vegan diet

I have consumed meat for as long as I can remember. I include all animal products in this, is guess. I love a good eggs benedict just as much as the next gal. So, when Wes and I watched a documentary about how animals are treated when manufactured for the sole purpose of feeding the masses—I was totally disgusted.

"How can they do that?" I asked, Wes.

"Seems weird, right?"

Weird was just the tip of the iceberg. According to the documentary, chickens were bred to have very quick growing cycles and breasts double the size of normal chickens. The new and improved chickens aren't able to carry their own weight, so they sit day after day in their own...well, you know...until that dreadful day they are transported to the butcher.

I didn't watch that portion of the documentary. (The slaughtering part.) I lied, and told Wes that I had to go to the bathroom. Seriously, there's only so much I can stomach.

The program ended and viewers were encouraged to eat organic meats, or to give up animal products altogether.

"Maybe we should try a vegan diet for a little while," I said, staring at the credits as they filled the television screen.

Wes was all for it. So, we were going to be vegans. We marched into the kitchen and pealed back the pantry doors. Holy Martha May Who! We had a ton of food that we were going to have to donate to a non-vegan family.

We started the new lifestyle with gusto! We went to the grocery store and purchased only organic produce and dried beans. We found some organic peanut butter and took the vegan supplies home.

I soaked the dried beans overnight and that Sunday morning, instead of having our normal bacon, eggs and toast...we had avocado, tomato and black bean salsa.

Mmmm, not so much!

One meal and I already missed my bacon. Around day five, I notice strange little changes to my body. Not weight loss, though. No, no it was a surplus of natural gas. My belly was so bloated that if I had lost any weight, no one would be the wiser.

I was miserable and irritable. I was frustrated with my lack of cooking skills when my menu only included black beans and rice.

There are only so many concoctions one can make. Well, for me anyway! I suppose I could have researched the vegan diet more extensively...or at all, but I didn't. Again, the impatience I am known for shines through. We were far too excited to get slowed down by research!

Day thirteen and I was at work when a pizza delivery was made. PIZZAAAH! I didn't care who ordered it, I didn't care if they charged me twenty dollars for a slice. I was going to get some animal products into my stomach.

I followed the scent of cheese and bacon until I came to the lunch room.

"I will give you five bucks for a slice of that pizza," I announced.

My co-worker looked at me and tilted his head.

"April, I thought you were a vegan?"

"Not anymore! I need meat!"

"Help yourself," he said, and laughed.

I chose the largest piece and stared intently at the clumps of sausage, bacon, ham, pepperoni and cheese. Usually, the old meat-eater me, would have taken a napkin and patted the top in an effort to soak up the excess grease. But, I was not longer that girl! I was craving the meat juices like a, like a...oh whatever! I took a huge bite and slowly chewed while enjoying the combination of flavors. Mmm, meat! Oooh, cheese! Awe, good night that's good!

I will not tell you what my consequences were, only to say that I was gurgling in the digestive area for the next two hours! At work! Of all the places to have *that* problem, right?

"I cheated today," I said, as I walked through the front door.

Wes stared at me in utter shock.

"I had meat!" I shouted. "I know, I know! Hang me from the rafters from my toes and sacrifice my impure body to the vegetable gods!"

I saw a smile slowly spread across his lips. His nose scrunched up a little on the left side and he said, "I did too!"

"Seriously! Oh thank goodness! I thought you were going to be all disappointed in me. I mean, we both know I don't have the patience to really think things through. I know I should have purchase a cookbook, or printed off some recipes. Do you think we should research it more?" I was hoping for a *no*. What he said was even better!

"No way! I can't keep eating black beans and pretending like it's my favorite food!" Wes replied, shaking his head.

That night we ate steak! Oh my land! It was the best, tenderest, melt-in-your-mouth steak I have ever had.

We need to stop watching
documentaries!

Juice your way to health

Welcome to the Elder

movie night. It was Friday and we were flipping through the random list of new releases when we came across yet another documentary! Surprised, right? This one was about detoxing with juice.

Juicing! It's the latest trend in Hollywood and with people who watch too many stinking documentaries. Grab your popcorn and a juicer...here we go again.

"Ha," I laughed, as we were waiting in the checkout line. "How many times do you think this cashier has seen the same thing?"

"You mean, a grocery cart filled with fruits, vegetables and a juicer?"

I nodded.

"Probably a hundred times today," he sighed.

After spending nearly $200 and loading my poor little trunk to its maximum weight limit in apples, oranges, ginger, lemons and pears we went to lunch.

"I guess this is our last meal for a few days, huh?" I asked, as the waitress put the menus on the table.

"Better make it good," Wes said, as he smiled up at the girl.

Good gravy! We ordered so much food it was ridiculous!

"I will have the monster-cheese-onion-mushroom burger with a side of onion rings. Oh, and can we get the pretzel bites and some fried pickles for an appetizer?" I asked.

"I will have the teriyaki-bacon-swiss-peppered-jack burger and tater tots," Wes said. "Oh, and can I get a side of ranch dressing too?"

"Oh, yeh I would like ranch as well," I spouted.

Why is it that when you are going to start a new diet, you decide that you will never, ever eat anything from a restaurant again? Did we really believe this was going to be the last high-calorie, full-fat meal we were ever going to have?

Well, yeh! Sheesh, this was it! This was the diet that was to change everything! We both knew it.

After gorging ourselves to the point of total discomfort we made the drive home. I was feeling the effects of the fried pickles and may have tooted. Normally, I don't do that in Wes's company, but I was so uncomfortable from all of the food I ate. Here's the deal, we have been married for more than sixteen years. A slip every once in a while is normal, right?

"Holy crap!" Wes exclaimed, as he turned his head toward me.

"What?"

"Can't you smell that?"

I started giggling which quickly turned into a full belly laugh.

In between dramatic gasps of air, he rolled down the window and I apologized in between chuckles.

"I'm sorry," I said. "I didn't think it was going to be that bad!"

"Baby, you need to clean that out!"

"Well, get me home and let's get juicing," I said, trying my best to be serious.

Excitement built as we unloaded the car. The juicer was out of the box and in the sink filled with suds, while Wes was chopping fruits and vegetables.

"Hey," I said. "Look, the juicer came with a recipe book!"

"Bonus," Wes said, and took the book from my soapy hands.

It is a good thing the juicer came with recipes because, I am sure you have already guessed it...I didn't research the art of juicing. Once again, we were sailing ships in unchartered territory. The blind leading the blind, so to speak. But, we were committed this time. We were going to juice ourselves skinny!

We assembled the juicer in seconds and we were ready for our first juice concoction. Wes had picked out a recipe and had all of the ingredients ready to go. We positioned the machine and began feeding it oranges.

Fruit and vegetable were being turned into juice right before our eyes. Lemons, carrots, celery, ginger, apples, pears. You name it, the machine digested it in seconds.

"Spinach?" I asked, as Wes filled the tube with a handful of greens.

"It's what the recipe said," he shrugged, and pushed the plunger down forcing a river of green gelatinous looking liquid to flow from the machine.

"Now," he said, as he turned the juicer off, "Now we put it in the blender and add a banana."

"Really?"

So, off to the other side of the kitchen we went with a large pitcher full of pea-soup-colored juice. Into the blender with a banana and after a few vrooms of the blades, we had our first juice recipe completed.

"It smells good," Wes said, pouring the liquid into two large glasses.

"Cheers," I said, holding my glass up to the light. I took a very small sip.

"Not bad at all! I can't even taste the spinach in there," I said.

"Mmm, me either. So, how often are we supposed to drink these?"

Huh, good question.

Anyone?

Anyone?

Yeh, me either!

Time for an Internet search.

"Every two-to-three hours," I yelled, from the office.

"Wow! That's a lot of juicing," Wes said, from the kitchen.

Day one of our new juice diet was a success. I mean, we completed it and didn't feel too bad by the end of the day. Although, I think we were both a little surprised by the amount of fruits and vegetables we ingested.

Day two started off with Wes and I walking around the house feeling like we had been out all night drinking shots. Our heads were pounding and we were literally pushing one another out of the hallway to get to the bathroom. Things were working, obviously, but why did we feel so horrible?

Internet! Search: Juicing side-effects

Results (as I understood them): Juicing, according to many health care professionals, rids your body of toxins.

Okay, that sounds like a good thing.

Juicing can also cause hangover-like symptoms because the liver and kidneys are bombarded with new minerals to expel from the body.

Lovely!

Many doctors do not recommend juicing for more than three consecutive days.

Ugh, two more days of this?

While others recommend a single day of juicing to jump-start the body into a natural detox.

Now we're talking!

I inform Wes of my research findings and we decide, together, that one day of juicing was enough. We spent the following month juicing only for breakfast and only on work days. I must admit, having one glass of healthy juiced greens in the morning was much easier than trying to choke a glass down every two hours.

After about a month, the novelty wore off and we stored the juicer away. Anyone need a juicer for a great price?

I grew up on two-percent milk and white bread.

But, but... sugar is my friend

I like sugar! I like coffee with sugar, cookies with sugar, soda with sugar, bread with butter and sugar...I like sugar! Okay, now that we have that out of the way, guess what we did last Friday night? Yup, we watched another documentary! This one was about refined stuff.

According to this documentary, guess what is the worst thing you can eat? Yup, you guessed it! SUGAR!

Not brown sugar, no, no the pure white manmade sugar I digest on a very regular basis. Why is it so bad, you may wonder? Well, according to the scientists and doctors in the show, it is refined therefore, our unrefined caveman (or cavewoman) bodies haven't quite figured out a way to process it.

So, according to the (I am sure they are actual doctors) our body produces fat cells to surround the little white sugar cells to protect the rest of our body from them. Like an army of fat cells on a mission to make me fat!

What the...seriously? Freak! We really need to stop watching documentaries!

Help me people!

Help me stop the insanity!

So, knowing we have tried and failed (how many times?) after watching a food-related show, wouldn't you think that by now, Wes and I would realize that we are simply going to try and fail at this? One might think that, but after watching the said show...we got all pumped up like pro-wrestlers and started changing what we put into our bodies.

"No more white stuff," I announced, after the show concluded.

"Deal," Wes conceded.

Do I have to even tell you how this adventure ended? Badly! Very, very badly!

We started the white-free diet on Saturday.

Of course we did.

Together.

Ready?

The first thing I do every morning is brew coffee. The second thing I do each morning is use the bathroom. Priorities, right? Well, according to the latest revelation in weight loss, black coffee and tea are approved items. Yay! Here's the kicker folks, I drink sugar-coffee! What I mean is, I put more sugar than coffee into my little cup.

There was a time when I couldn't even stand the smell of coffee. That was in my twenties when I preferred wine coolers to actual wine. Yes, my taste has seriously evolved over the last seventeen years, or so. When I started drinking coffee it had to have sugar and milk. When I met Wes, we had the milk conversation during our first trip to the grocery store.

"Yuck, two-percent milk?" Wes asked, as I placed the gallon into the shopping cart.

"Yeh, what kind of milk do you drink?" I asked.

Now remember, we were newlyweds. So naïve and so in love that a conversation about milk was as exciting as, well, I suppose as exciting as shopping for socks. Everything in our relationship was new.

"Fat-free," he said, pointing the gallon with the light-blue cap.

After much debate, we comprised and purchased a half gallon of each. We had the same dilemma in the bread aisle. I grew up on white bread and Wes grew up with wheat bread.

Thinking I was being a good wife, I chose to go with the wheat bread. It is healthier, right?

So, we had pretty much cut out white flour during our first month of marriage which meant, for this new diet expose', we were really just concentrating on eliminating white sugar.

I poured myself a cup of very black coffee and made my way to the office. I powered up the computer and tried to slurp down the bitter liquid. Total failure. I needed sugar. So, rather than sneaking into the kitchen and pouring eight rounded tablespoons of sugar into my cup I set it down in the sink. I returned to my laptop and played a few games.

Then it happened! It took about thirty minutes for my body to react.

Boom, boom, boom.

I could feel my heart beating in my temples. It felt like my forehead was going to explode! Wes was in the living room nursing some black tea.

"I think I am going to die," I said, and plopped down next to him.

"A little dramatic, don't you think?"

"Seriously? No, my head feels like it is going to blow up!"

Just so you know, Wes quit eating sugar about three months before and switched to a not-real-sugar substitute. His happy time lasted for about another fifteen minutes before his body realized what was happening. It wasn't getting any more not-real-sugar!

"What is up with my head?" He asked, as he reclined in the chair. His forearm was resting on his forehead.

"Death. I am telling you, we are going to die from sugar withdrawals."

We spent the entire day in our pajamas, in the recliners commiserating about how badly we had been treating our bodies.

At 7:30 that night, we retired to our bed. The next morning we awoke and stared blankly at the coffee maker. Our headaches had gone away over the course of sleeping and thankfully, we were both feeling a whole lot better.

"I don't really like black coffee," I said.

"Me either."

We cleaned out the coffee maker and put it in the cupboard. We made it three hours without caffeine before our heads were once again pounding to the beat of their own drums.

"I will get the coffee maker," he said, as he was walking toward the kitchen.

"I will get the sugar," I replied.

We waited and watched the coffee drip slowly into the carafe. I swear we were each drooling as we measured our sugar and fake-sugar into our clean coffee mugs.

Heads still pulsating, we sat in our respective recliners and drank from the cup of life. It took two cups each to kill the monsters in our heads.

We vowed, to one another, to stop watching documentaries and start eating better foods. All foods, not just one kind.

I also decided to do some research into body detoxing...the correct method.

Inspiration to lose the weight
came in the form of a book.

Lifestyle change

There is a difference between being lazy verses being unmotivated. There is also a difference between inspiration and motivation. I have struggled to find the right mix of healthy and easy.

What I have learned is this:

If it is easy...it doesn't work! Not only in weight loss, but life in general. If something promises to be so good that you question it, more often than not you have to go with your gut feeling.

The same stands for weight loss. I can't just purchase a juicer and have six glasses of fabulous fruits and veggies, thinking the scale is going to reveal a huge weight loss.

The same goes for changing your diet before speaking to your doctor or, at the very least, researching the diet itself.

Like I said in the last chapter, as soon I revealed that I was trying to lose weight everyone had a plan for me. But, their plan, the one that worked wonders for them, didn't interest me at all.

I needed something I could believe in. Something I could really commit too and finding that solution took a lot of time and research.

Oh! And did I mention we watched another documentary? (Of course we did!) Needless to say, after watching the documentary, I said nothing to Wes. I went into my office and searched the infamous Internet for "Foods to eat in order to lose weight."

Rather than the expected links to blogs and Wiki, I found an innocent looking book with a very clear title: Clean. The book was written by a cardiologist, so I downloaded it. I read it cover to cover and found my inspiration for living a cleaner life.

This was the moment I decided to take control of my life and my out-of-control weight. (I am not suggesting this book will inspire you. Each one of us is different in our quest to find balance and happiness. For me, this was the final push I needed to get the ball rolling.)

I won't go into the whole book, but the concept was pretty simple and clean. Cut out the processed and refined foods. Eat whole foods and meats without hormones or antibiotics.

What I really liked about the idea was, it made sense to me. It clicked, the little light bulb illuminated above my head and I was suddenly committed in a way I never had been before. This didn't seem like all of the other times I had seen something or read something. This was a full body, mind and spirit detoxification.

Okay, enough about my inspiration, good grief! I sound like one of *those people* who have a weight loss program for you to try! Honestly, if you are ready to lose weight, gain insight on your own health, and live happier, find your own inspiration and then never give up. The Fat Suit does not own me and yours surely doesn't own you. It doesn't define us. It doesn't define us. Empower yourself to find what will work. I can tell you what did for me, but what if it doesn't for you? I know how it feels to fail and I do not want to be responsible for causing you those feelings.

It took me a long time. Geeze, it took me over ten years to finally find something that made sense. Lord knows I tried and failed many times while on my quest.

Here we go again.

The last time

Can I really be patient enough? Can I really go through with a lifestyle change (yet, again) and not get frustrated when I wake up the following morning to this Fat Suit? I have given myself permission to fail so many times in the past.

This time was different though.

I had goals! I had plans! I had prepared! Three very important things for sure. Do you know what was, for me, the most important of all of these? I was tired of being tired. I was sick of being sick.

I was committed to make this work! I wanted, more than anything, to walk in front of a mirror again and not feel lazy, fat, ugly, or self-conscience. I wanted to look at candid photos without cringing. I wanted to be the old me. The one that could care less what others thought. I wanted to just feel better!

This was it!

Part of the problem with my previous attempts was I had not really prepared for the changes. Sure, I cleaned out the pantry, but I didn't think about replacing the items with healthier choices. Instead, we felt as though we were starving or eating one specific type of food for weeks.

Not this time!

I cleaned out the pantry, turning every package over in my hand and read the ingredients. If there was sugar, high-fructose corn syrup, refined flour or a word that I couldn't pronounce: straight into a box for the local soup kitchen.

I did the same with the refrigerator. Surprisingly, most of the condiments in the fridge were either passed their use-by date, or they contained what I considered: off-limit ingredients.

Why do we keep mayonnaise bottles that are four months past the use-by date? Why did I have so many expired things in the door of my fridge? The more I looked through the contents, the more I realized we hadn't used a lot of the stuff for quite some time. But, we were hoarding it...maybe so the fridge didn't look bare? I have no idea, but it felt great to actually clean out every nook and cranny. I swear, my fridge has never been cleaner. Well, at least not since it was delivered and brand new!

I reorganized my kitchen cabinets and spice rack. I moved my storage containers to a more convenient area and took an inventory of the spices I had.

I placed the juicer near the sink and found a large bowl for fruit. I dedicated a knife and cutting board to juicing and placed them beside the juicer.

The blender, crockpot and mixer I put on the counter and then retreated to my office.

There, I made a list. A very long list of things I would need from the farmers market, from the grocery store and from the big-box stores. I included items that I had read in the book, like flaxseed and kale.

I went to each of the stores and almost passed out at the checkout counter each time. Eating and living better was much more expensive than living out of cans and pre-packaged meals.

Then I had a thought. I was eating out five days a week for lunch. I was drinking two to three, twenty-four ounce white mochas six days a week and we ate out for dinner at least once a week. Oh! And then there were the nights one of us would stop and pick up fast food for dinner because neither of us wanted to cook.

Hmm, maybe eating better wasn't more expensive.

Okay, here we go. Time to get home and revamp everything I have come to know as unhealthy.

Preparation is the key to success.

Ready? Set. Wait!

Half of the battle was done. I had cleaned out and reorganized the counters, refrigerator and cabinets. I had prepared my kitchen and dedicated items for a healthier lifestyle. I had shopped until I thought I was going to drop and stared at my countertops filled with brightly-colored, fresh food.

Now what?

I knew I had to make a plan. A food plan. I drive by nine fast food establishments every night on my way home from work. I needed to construct a menu before Monday morning to ensure that I was prepared for the week ahead.

I did just that! I planned our meals by two. Whatever I made for dinner, I would make double. That way, we were certain to have lunch the following day. It wasn't that much more work. I followed the menu every night and packaged up our lunches before serving our dinner.

I figured we should eat less for dinner and more for lunch. It took some patience and that first week, and there were a couple of days our dinner wasn't all that wonderful, which meant our lunches the next day weren't going to be as enjoyable. But, I learned, and I continued to cook every night.

At first, Wes had to jazz everything up with hot sauce. Our taste buds were not used to the natural flavors. The food was "too clean." By week two, something changed. For both of us. We found that we didn't need extra seasonings in our meals. We found that we were getting full faster and we were craving fresh over processed foods.

I gave up my morning latte and replaced it with fresh juice. I also started eating breakfast for the first time since I was in high school!

Simple breakfast: old fashioned oats, slivered almonds and coconut milk.

Throughout the afternoon, I would drink water. I found it energizing...even more so than my old standby white mocha.

I started to wonder what my poor barista thought. I used to see her three times a day. There was a part of me that wanted to drive through and tell her what I was doing. Then part of me knew I would order my drink and be right back to three a day in no time at all. I didn't want to jeopardize my progress. I made a deal that I would stop by and see her as soon as I had lost fifty pounds. By then, I figured, I would be confident and I wouldn't be tempted to fall back into my old routine.

It was around week three that our bodies experienced some changes. With all of the fruits, vegetables, and the depletion of sugars and processed foods—we found that things were flowing more smoothly—if you get my hint. Our bodies seemed to be handling the changes in a positive and regular way.

Encouraged by our progress, I went to the store and purchased a bathroom scale. I know, the forbidden giver of truth! But, as you now know, I gained weight everywhere and I wasn't feeling any lighter. I needed to know if what we were doing was assisting with my goal of losing seventy-five pounds.

I will tell you, I haven't owned a bathroom scale in nearly eight years. I have never been a fan of them, especially in my own house!

I won't leave you hanging!

Not wearing a bikini...yet

Change is never easy. But, after standing buck naked on the scale and reading, two-hundred and four pounds, I was convinced that we were on the right path.

For so many years I had been trying—in vain—to mask what it was that I didn't like about myself. I tried to love myself inside the Fat Suit. I did. But each day I saw my reflection was a day I was reminded of how truly unhappy I was. I couldn't see past the woman in the reflection. In my mind, I have always felt smaller—like the Fat

Suit never existed—but, reality wouldn't go away! Deep down, I knew I needed to lose the weight.

Now, ten pounds was a great start. I was encouraged and focused on not only how my body looked, but how it felt. I felt better, I walked taller and, although I still had that negative inner monologue...the constant inner criticism was decreasing.

I stopped dragging myself into the house at night after work and plopping down like a ragdoll in the recliner. I found that I was excited and raced to the kitchen to cook! I looked forward to making our juices and couldn't believe how much natural energy I had. This compared to the energy I used to have drinking two, to three, twenty-four ounce lattes every single day. I was sleeping more soundly and awakening feeling refreshed.

Even my skin was looking healthier. The large pores around my nose were visibly smaller. I hadn't seen Ted for quite some time and I had to wonder if I was the one providing him with the environment he needed to haunt my face.

Rather than turning on the television, I found myself listening to music and doing housework while Wes was outside mowing the lawn. I would dance around like a silly teenage girl with a sponge in one hand and an invisible microphone in the other. I am sure I looked like a complete mental case, but it felt good to move again.

Hey! I never complained about those.

Not the boobs!

Son of a!

Seriously?

My bras didn't fit anymore!

Okay, let me clarify that. They fit around me, but the cups were too big. I had a very large "pocket" between the top fabric of my bra and the flesh of my breasts.

Dang it! Of all the places I wanted to lose weight...the twins were not one (or two) of them.

What the heck?

Alright, time to inventory the rest of my body. Back to the mirror...**naked!**

No, I did not take a before picture of my naked self. Ugh. My luck, the photo would have accidentally been uploaded on the internet and, oh geez.

Someone asked me to see a before photo and I showed them my driver's license! It's not like I have any candid shots left.

Back to the bathroom. I undressed and felt that oh-so-familiar feeling of fear, regret, anticipation and somehow I just knew I was going to be disappointed in what I was about to see.

I took a deep breath and exhaled slowly through my nose in an attempt to prepare my mind for the new image of me. I closed my eyes and turned around to face the mirror straight on. Another deep breath and I opened my eyes.

Nothing! I noticed absolutely no difference in how my body looked in the mirror. My belly and boobs were in proportion to one another so trying to decipher if either is smaller could only be proved by the loose fit of my bra. Obviously, both had lost a little.

I shrugged my shoulders and saw the faint outline of my collar bones. I shrugged again, holding my shoulders up and traced the very obvious lines.

My collar bones are coming back!

I stared at my hands and began to notice the little fat pockets on my knuckles were shrinking and my wrist bones were actually protruding once more. I stopped the inspection there. I was encouraged by what I saw enough to know if I focused on my belly, I would become discouraged.

Losing the Fat Suit was going to take time. I had to be patient and silently celebrate each new discovery as it presented itself.

I put my clothes on, skipped to the kitchen and drank a big glass of water. The changes were working and I was on my way to skinny-vile.

Deciding to cheat for one day.

Super Bowl Sunday

"I don't think we should try to stick to our approved list of foods for the party," I said, as Wes walked into the living room.

"Really?" he asked.

"No, we have been doing great and really, what can one day hurt?"

Oh my gosh! We arrived at my sister's house to find a surplus of off-limit foods. Foods that Wes and I once ate in overabundance. Little smokies bathed in BBQ sauce and grape jelly, 9-layer bean dip, fried tortilla chips, homemade salsa and guacamole dip! Clam dip with potato chips, no-bake cookies, cupcakes, pizza roll ups made from crescent rolls...dear Lord, I was on overload!

I grabbed a large plate—even though small plates were offered—and began loading a scoop of everything. The plate began to crease under the weight. I topped it off with a handful of chips and proudly presented it to Wes. He smiled.

I sat down and stared at my selections. I wanted to devour the entire plate in one single bite but, I was aware of the other people around me. I needed to stay calm, cool and collected.

I speared a smokie with my fork and slowly placed it into my mouth. I waited for the flavors to hit my palette. I inhaled deeply through my nose. It tasted wonderful! Better than any little smokie I had ever experienced. The same was true about the clam dip and chips. I felt amazing. I felt like I was in Hog Heaven.

I cleaned up the last remnants of dip with a chip and returned to the kitchen for a cookie. I grabbed two and had the first one swallowed before returning to my seat in the living room. The game had started and all of the attention was on the upcoming commercials. (Okay, Wes wanted his team to win the game, but all I really cared about was the commercials.)

Everything quickly became a blur. The television was fuzzy and the room was spinning at light speed. My stomach was on overload and gasses began forming deep within me. I could feel popping and gurgling. I knew what was next.

My head started to pound ferociously. I could feel sweat beginning to form on my brows. My heart rate increased. Surely, I wasn't going to have a heart attack? It was only a few little smokies.

Halftime came and went. I was praying Wes would want to leave early since the game was a total shut out and his team was destined for the ring. When I looked over at him, he was engrossed watching, yelling and cheering on his beloved Hawks.

So much for leaving anytime soon.

The rumbling and bubbling continued to build until the game was finally over. I grabbed Wes's plate and threw it into the garbage. I apologized to my sister for not staying and helping her clean up, but I had to go. I really had to go!

"Holy crap," Wes exclaimed, as we both got into the car. "I haven't felt this sick to my stomach in a long time."

"Seriously? I thought I was the only one? Why didn't you tell me?" I asked, buckling my seatbelt.

"Why do you wear your seatbelt when we are only going an eighth of a mile?" he asked.

"Habit, I guess." The gurgling continued and I rubbed my stomach.

"You looked like you were having fun," he replied, to my earlier question.

"Fun? Huh. Anything but, my friend. I have been sitting in pain for the past two hours just hoping this would pass."

He laughed. "Oh, it'll pass alright."

It did. It passed so many times that we decided that our next home improvement project was going to be installing a second bathroom.

Three hours later, we were sitting and staring blankly at the television.

"I can't believe we got so sick," I said.

"Who would have thought that our bodies would have forgotten so quickly? We ate like that, well not quite like that, but we used to eat that stuff all of the time."

"I know," I said. I reached out and grabbed his hand.

"No more cheating," he said.

"Agreed!"

That was the last time we gorged ourselves. It was not the last time we cheated, but we were more cautious. We ate smaller portions of the forbidden foods, and waited to see how badly our bodies would react before commencing.

The scale is broken.

Plateau

For two weeks, the scale read the same. Not a single pound lost, but not a single pound gained either. I guess I should have been grateful, but honestly I was frustrated. I wanted so badly to lose the Fat Suit quickly. I wanted to fall asleep and awaken to a new me. A much smaller me and although I knew the scale is not really broken, I wanted to blame it.

I was still eating right and juicing. I wasn't cheating...not after the way I felt after the Super Bowl Party!

Why wasn't I losing any weight?

I promised Wes when we purchased the scale that I wouldn't become obsessed with it. I had promised him that I would only weigh myself once per week. After two weeks of seeing the exact same number appear, I broke my promise to Wes and began obsessing.

I stood on the stupid thing every morning before I took a shower. I silently prayed each time that the number would be less than what it was the day before.

Have you every stared at a pot waiting for it to boil? Very frustrating isn't it? That is exactly how I felt every morning. Day after day for fourteen days I experienced the same outcome. No weight loss, no weight gain. I had to do something to get the scale moving in the right direction.

Crunches and pushups! That was my solution. I decided to do as many crunches and pushups as I could every morning when Wes left the house for work. I started with twenty-five crunches and felt the muscles tighten. I was shocked when I did seventy-five crunches that first morning. I was right. I did have some muscles under all of that bubble wrap!

Next were pushups. I got into position— the girl pushup position—and made it to three partial pushups before my arms began to shake violently. So, three pushups. Three was better than none, right?

I worked my way up to one-hundred and fifty crunches and fifteen pushups before the scale moved again. I had lost two whopping pounds in two weeks. Two stupid pounds!

Time for research.

What is the worst exercise—according to the Internet—to do if you are trying to lose belly fat? Yup, you guessed it...crunches!

Oh for crying out loud! Someone throw me a bone here!! (And not a "big bone.")

Progress is progress.

Never imagined

I thought about giving up. I did! But, then I would get out a pair of size sixteen pants and put them on and stare at myself in front of the mirror. No, no. I did not want to go back there...ever, ever again. Undoubtedly, losing the Fat Suit had been the hardest thing I have ever attempted.

This, coming from a thirty-eight year old woman who decided to go to college three years ago to get a two year degree! I work fulltime too and of course, write pages and pages of random thoughts that may eventually get combined into a book.

Attending college, working, writing, and still finding time for my husband and family was challenging. But, even more so was maintaining the commitment I had made to myself to lose the Fat Suit. There were many afternoons when I wanted a sweetened coffee. There were birthday celebrations at work, and I am not going to lie...the cupcakes looked and smelled delicious!

My dear husband had lost all the weight he had set out to. I still had more to go. Why is it men can lose weight so much faster than women? I know, random. But, I look at him and he is muscular, tall and fit. He didn't have to run a mile everyday...in fact, all he had to do was eat and drink what I made for him. What a total cheater! I am kidding of course. I could not have come this far in my weight loss without his support and encouragement.

It is funny really. Not ha, ha funny, but funny in a more ironic way. Wes has always insisted that I am beautiful at any weight. When we started the journey, he actually saw changes in me long before I did.

"I don't want you to take this the wrong way," he said, as he walked into the kitchen.

I was in the process of chopping vegetables for dinner.

"What?" I asked, cautiously.

"The lump on the back of your neck is gone," he said and he placed his hand on the upper portion of my back.

"I had a lump?"

"Well, more like a fat roll, I guess," he said.

Seriously?

"It's gone, though," he said, with a little pride in his voice.

"What else?" I asked.

From there, Wes told me about the things he had noticed on my body. There were a lot of little changes that he had noticed that I had not. While the conversation was awkward, to say the least, I appreciated him *noticing.* I was absolutely stunned at the changes he pointed out. He was right! My body was slimming down and although it wasn't quick or obvious, the little things he brought to my attention really helped keep me on track.

I felt empowered. Like I could take on anything! So, what was one thing I needed to kick in order to really have a healthier life? The one dirty little secret I have had for the past nineteen years? The one thing that is holding me back from a true cardio workout?

Yup, I am a smoker! Half a pack per day! I know, if you are a smoker, you are reading this and thinking:

Seriously, you are not a smoker! Smokers smoke three packs a day. You're just a wannabe smoker!

Okay, so no one was really going to chastise me for smoking eight-to-ten cigarettes everyday. But, I knew I needed to quit. So, I did.

I purchased my last pack of smokes and told myself when they were gone, I was done. Uh—I did buy a second pack when that one was getting low—I wasn't quite ready to quit at that point.

I did though. It took me three days longer than I thought (because of the additional pack). But, hey, I was getting somewhere. The last cigarette wasn't as ceremonious as I thought it would have been. I mean—it was my last one. Actually, I thought I had one more in the pack when I took out that one. So, I puffed like I had one more left. Nonchalantly, not really taking in the flavors—who was I kidding? It was a cigarette, not a fine cigar.

Anyway, three hours later, I went to grab my last cigarette and realized the pack was empty. I said some cuss words, squeezed the paper pack with all my muscle might, and tossed it into the garbage can.

I had a nervous foot for three days. It would tap, shake, quiver and roll around of its own accord. I started to drink a large glass of water each time I felt the urge to light up and discovered my urges were becoming less and less after the first four days. Thank goodness, because my co-workers were beginning to think I had a bladder infection!

Was it easy?

Are you kidding?

This whole process of weight loss and healthy living lifestyle has been one of the most difficult things I have done in my thirty-eight years of life. I'll be completely honest though, I do miss smoking more than I miss ice cream!

Author note

I fell off the wagon! I started smoking again. It was Saturday morning and I had just finished cleaning the wood floors of our house. I was trapped in the kitchen with nothing to do for about five minute. Usually, I would step outside to have a cigarette and wait for the floors to dry.

That morning? Yeh, I caught myself eating a juice pulp cookie. (Recipe is in the back of the book.) Now, the cookies aren't bad for you, but the fact that I was eating it out of shear boredom freaked the living crap out of me. Before I knew what was happening, I was on my second—not bite—cookie!

One of my greatest fears was I would quit smoking and replace that habit with food. I had seen others do it. So, what did I do? Well, I pulled my hair in a ponytail, walked across the nearly dried floor, drove to the nearest convenient store and purchased a pack of smokes.

I wish I could tell you that it was the best darn cigarette I had ever had, but the truth is...it wasn't. I felt like I had let myself down. I mean, here I was treating my body like a temple and feeding it whole organic foods. I was losing weight and so proud of my progress. Why was it I couldn't kick this habit?

"What happened?" Wes asked. He could smell the foul odor as soon as I walked into the living room. He has never been a fan of the smell.

"I was eating. I was eating because I was waiting for the floor to dry," I replied. I lowered my head in shame.

"April, it is 10:30 in the morning. Maybe you were eating because you were hungry."

"I don't think so," I said. "I was waiting for the floors to dry and before I realized what was happening, I was shoveling food into my mouth!"

"Honey, I understand how hard this is for you to quit smoking, I do. Nicotine will probably be harder for you to kick than anything else you have ever done," he said.

I nodded in agreement.

"But," he continued, "I don't want you to use it as a crutch. You can't keep smoking for fear you are going to gain weight."

"That is exactly what I am afraid of! I don't get it, Wes. I know better, I do. But, the voice inside my head is telling me that I am going to replace that bad habit with one just as bad for me."

"You won't. You are too stubborn," he said, with a smile.

"I'm sorry," I replied.

"Why?"

"Because I let you down. I know how much you hate my smoking. I know how much you wanted me to quit," I said.

Wes stood up and wrapped his arm around me.

"You stink," he said.

"I know, and I know that smoking is bad for my health. I know that I am detoxing my body of all the chemicals in food, but replacing it with even more toxins and carcinogens by smoking. I know all of this! Why can't I get my brain on board?"

"You will. When you are ready, you will. Until then, though, go and brush your teeth!"

I'm so naïve.

This is the easy part?

I know people mean well. I do. But, really?

I was two-and-a-half months committed to our healthier lifestyle when I was caught off guard by an innocent conversation over dinner with friends.

"April, seriously, losing the weight is the easy part!"

WHAT? I'm sorry, can we re-read that last sentence?

"April, seriously, losing the weight is the easy part!"

Easy?

They think this has been easy?

"You are joking right?" I asked.

"Not at all! The hardest part will be for you to keep the weight off."

"You think for one minute, I am going to get down to the weight I feel good at and I am going to jeopardize it by…how?" I asked.

"95% of all diets fail and people not only gain the original weight back, but additional weight as well," they said, with conviction.

Now, I have heard this. In fact, I have experienced this with my previous attempts. But now?

"But, I am not on a diet. I have changed my way of thinking, cooking and even eating foods," I argued.

"It's a diet," she said. "The key will be to keep the weight off once you get to your ideal weight. And trust me! It is very difficult to do."

It is?

I stewed over the words on and off during the meal and even during the drive home. How was losing the weight going to be easier than maintaining? It just didn't make any logical sense to me.

If, let's say, I get down to a size seven pants. Wouldn't it be obvious if said pants started to get a little snug? Wouldn't that be a sign I needed to make a little tweak?

I had spent ten years living inside a Fat Suit! Could I ever forget that? Could I ever delete the picture in my mind of my naked body at forty-five degrees? Could I forget how I felt each time I saw the real me in a picture?

Don't listen to the negative, I told myself, fighting hard against my negative inner-voice.

I wasn't dieting. I wasn't trying to lose weight for a family reunion. I wasn't trying to lose weight for a guy. I wasn't trying to lose weight for anyone else!

Just me.

I wasn't doing a fad diet. I wasn't eating special, premade foods. I wasn't taking a large amount of supplements or addition vitamins. I wasn't doing anything but eating whole fruits and whole vegetables. I was juicing, and I was trying to purchase organic grass fed meats. Which was difficult to find but, I was determined, and I succeeded more often than not.

This journey didn't feel like a diet. I felt like I was saving myself from a future filled with disappointment and unhappiness. I wasn't one of those women who liked what the mirror offered. I wasn't proud of my body. I didn't wear tight t-shirts or even shorts because I was embarrassed by the way I looked. I didn't own a swimsuit. Even if I did, I wouldn't wear it anywhere! (Seriously...we have a hot tub in our backyard, and I haven't stepped foot in it in over four years!)

I was the girl who laughed about her weight. I was the girl who secretly wished she had caught herself when her size five jeans got tight and started exercising. I didn't, though, and now I am the girl in the Fat Suit!

I went to the doctor for my yearly check up on March 14, 2014. I asked to be weighed! (I know, right?) I stood on the scale and read one-hundred-eighty-nine pounds. I smiled.

"Good for you," the nurse said.

"Thanks," I replied.

"Wow, you have lost forty pounds since your last appointment."

"Forty? I thought my starting weight was two-hundred-fourteen pounds?"

"Um, December 23, 2013, your weight was two-hundred and twenty –nine pounds," she said. A warm smile spread across her lips.

Yup! I am on my way to losing the Fat Suit. I don't think I will ever forget what it felt like living in it for so long. I will enjoy looking into the mirror and seeing the image that better represents how I feel about myself.

I will keep the Fat Suit forever in my mind. Once this book goes New York Best Seller and I am signing books at every bookstore in the U.S. and abroad—you will come and see me. You will see me without the Fat Suit. We will high-five and we will go to a coffee shop. Yes, yes we will! I will order a black coffee—no sweetener—and we chat about our successes and failures.

Or…you will find me in all black clothing trying in vain to cover the lumps and bumps that make up my fat suit. We will talk about our failed attempts. We will compare support garment choices, and I will have a white mocha filled with sugar! Either way…we will talk and laugh like high school girls in the bathroom!

This is not my favorite chapter. In fact, I chose to only include it in the paperback version!

Photo journal

In 1996, I weighed one-hundred-twelve pounds, and somehow believed that I was fat! I know, let's both find a time machine, go back and knock some sense into this anything but chunky chick!

Me, in early 2003. I had cut off my hair, dyed it brown and grew to a size ten.

In 2006, we took a vacation to Mexico. We decided to do a little zip-line adventure. I was sure the line was going to snap as soon as I latched on. It didn't, but I was miserable the entire trip.

I refused to wear shorts. I can tell you, Mexico is hot and humid—I was uncomfortable, but stuck to my guns. I may have lost a few pounds during the vacation, but I gained it back, plus some, after we returned home.

Remember, my weight gain didn't happen overnight. (I wrote this more for myself, because in my mind…it did! I woke up one morning to this!)

This photo was taken on Christmas morning. *Ugh*, this is why I don't like candid shots! This was my heaviest weight to date. I weighed two-hundred, twenty-nine pounds and I wore a size sixteen!

I know, I claimed to be a size twelve-ish this entire time. It was a lie! I tried so hard to convince myself that I peaked at just below average. Well, proof is in the pudding and Lord knows I had a lot of extra pudding.

This photo was taken after I had written the first draft of the book you are reading now. Yes, I gained even more weight! The original book stopped back on page one-hundred and thirteen-ish. I never thought that I would have the determination to put forth the effort to lose the Fat Suit. That was before I saw my reflection and the photo above. That was the moment I decided to continue on this journey, and include the possible failures along the way. No more crying in bed, no more wishing for a magical diet pill or dreaming of contracting mono. I needed to find a way to lose the Fat Suit and find true health.

"What are you doing?"

Don't take my word for it.

I did a radio interview mid-March to promote this book. The DJ asked me for the name of diet I was on. (Thankfully, the show was pre-recorded!)

"It's called, nottadiet," I replied.

"Now, how do you spell that?" she asked.

"Um—not a diet," I said, slowly.

"And where can our listeners find information on this program?"

"Uh—there is not program. It's not a diet," I said.

Silence filled the air. I felt kind of silly actually. Here I was trying to promote myself, but instead, I kind of came off a little—well dumb.

I have been asked what diet I am on by just about everyone at work, online and even my mom!

"April, Dana wanted me to ask you what diet you were following. I guess she saw some of your pictures on Facebook."

"Mom, tell Dana: it's nottadiet."

"Well, that's a weird name. Nottadiet huh? Well, I am so happy that it is working for you."

Okay, so rather than recreate the wheel or try to argue the obvious fact that I talk too fast! Let's just call this adventure I am on "Nottadiet."

I already said this isn't a how-to book. But, I hear you, and you want to know what I am doing to lose the fat suit. I will cave as long as you promise me you will do your research and not take my word on anything you are about to read. Promise? Okay...

The most important thing I have learned so far, it this: In order to change your entire belief system in regards to health, you must believe in the new system. I can write a step-by-step guide to how I lost the weight, but "what if?" There is so much information out there, what if I lead you astray? What if I missed something important in my research? I don't want to give you the exact steps I have taken. Instead...I would like to give you some insight and some tools. You have to decide what to believe in.

I don't want to set you up to fail. I would feel horrible. I mean, here we have come all this way. You've related to the stories and probably thought of your own along the way. I feel like we have bonded. We are friends. We are both tired of the fat suit. We are both looking in every possible place to find the zipper on the fat suit to no avail.

Just because I found the zipper, your zipper to the fat suit might be located elsewhere. I hope that makes sense. I realize it is a crazy analogy, but again...you have to find what works for you.

I made it personal. It's nottadiet that you can find anywhere.

Interesting discoveries

If it was made by a plant, we eat it. If it was made in a plant, we don't. It really is as simple and as complex as that, my friend.

I searched the internet and our local library for as many things health related as possible. I read about the latest diets and trends only to discover they all touted the same message. Cut out the garbage and eat whole foods.

Another thing I found of interest was the notion that our bodies are filled with harmful chemicals and products. Did you know that the

U.S. is one of very few nations that use artificial colors and flavorings? We want our food to look and taste great, but we don't stop to recognize the effects of these artificial components have on our insides.

Remember the cyst in my breast? I really didn't dwell too much on it in the chapter before, but I did a lot of research on the topic once I made the commitment to change my eating habits the cyst became smaller and smaller. During a self-exam on the third month, I realized I could barely feel it. It had gone from the size of an elongated lemon to the size of a penny!

Science has come a long way in improving the shelf-life of our foods and beverages. Science has also come a long way in developing sweeteners and preservatives. Our bodies however have not evolved at the same pace.

What does our body do with all of those new chemicals? Well, according to the research I did, it surrounds the foreign chemicals with mucus and stores it within our fat cells. Sometimes, depending on our diet, we begin to experience weight gain, sleeplessness and irritability. (Sound familiar?) We also experience inflammation.

One of the first things I noticed—after I began incorporating whole foods—was the bags under my eyes had disappeared. The puffiness in my hands that I had thought was fat had all but subsided as well. Remember when I was standing in front of the mirror and I ran my hands over my collar bones? They were not present, but were hidden beneath a squishy layer of fat. That squishy layer, I later found out, was the mucus my body had created to protect me from the unknown.

Inflammation is our bodies' natural reaction to protect us. The body will send out an army of cells to fight against the forces of evil. I guess I think of it like this: my army had been fighting and losing the fight for over ten years! My army was exhausted and never had a moment to rest because I wasn't allowing it the opportunity. When my army was tired, I was tired. I didn't sleep well because my body was still fighting against itself and the so called "nutrients" I had provided it.

The longer I fed my body chemicals and scientifically created junk, the less chance I had at a long vital life.

After reading...a lot...I became obsessed with the notion that I didn't want to get sick. The truth of the matter, though, I was already sick. I was in a constant state of unhealthy. My energy and focus transitioned from losing the fat suit, to losing the chemicals that had helped me to gain some of the weight in the beginning.

How many of you know someone who has lost a lot of weight and found themselves in the hospital with liver cancer or kidney stones? I have too! Those thoughts were never too far from my mind as I researched healthy alternatives.

How could I improve my health without causing so much of a drastic change that would shock my body and make me sick? Again, more research. (Now mind you, I was doing all of this before I started changing our lifestyle.)

Did you know, you always have the same amount of fat cells in your body? Rude, right? I thought the same thing! Rather than losing fat cells, they simply shrink. They never go away. I was beginning to understand why maintaining a specific weight could be more difficult than losing it in the first place.

So, if the fat cells, (which have been used by our body to store "the bad stuff") shrink...where does all of the bad stuff go? Ah-ha! It goes back into our bloodstream and triggers our little, worn out army all over again. UNLESS...you provide your body with some additional fire power!

I had read several articles on flax seeds and the benefits they provide for our body. Flax seeds are water soluble. Flax seeds create their own gel-like substance and once you digest them, you will see and feel the difference in your body.

(Try this: take a spoonful of flax seeds and place them in a glass with a spoonful of water. Leave them overnight and check out what happens.)

It was amazing! Instead of my body having to make mucus, I was providing it with a natural source! The flax seeds, (according to my research) carried the toxins out of my body through the intestinal wall. So, I was detoxing and removing the "bad stuff" which, hopefully, would keep me out of the hospital!

The more research I did the more discoveries I made. It was empowering! I felt like, for the first time in ten years, I had the key to my own health! I wasn't following any diet. I was making it up based on my needs and goals.

It is not failure if it was planned.

Cheating on purpose

Yes, I have cheated. No, I haven't failed. There is a different mindset when you cheat on purpose. No, no...I am not talking about cheating on Wes! Good Lord, after everything he has put up with? I would be a complete idiot to cheat on him! What I am talking about is eating foods that I know are not good for me.

Rather than locking myself in the house and refusing to eat a meal in a restaurant, I make the conscious decision to cheat. Fear of failure...like the one time I tried to quit smoking...has held me back so many times in the past. I would "fall off the wagon" and concede defeat. I would give up and return to my old unhealthy habits.

A few weeks ago, Wes and I went to a fast food restaurant for lunch. I knew I was going to cheat! There was no way I was going to limit myself to a salad without dressing. Give yourself the opportunity to eat the foods you used to eat all of time, but don't fall into the old habit of eating them everyday.

So, I ordered my old standby. It was a total let down! Like Super Bowl Sunday, I was expecting the food to taste as good as I remembered. It didn't taste good. It smelled like oil and left a thick residue in my mouth and on my teeth. Ick! My head started pounding with such immense force after about a half of an hour. My body was telling me: "We don't like this!"

Wes didn't feel too hot either.

"How could our body forget so quickly?" he asked, while rubbing his temple area.

"I don't know," I replied. "But, it definitely is not happy right now."

If you cheat, on purpose, and your body doesn't feel like crap...you haven't detoxed all of the toxins from your system. Once you remove all of the chemicals and junk, your body will retaliate against you! It was in the form of headaches, flatulent bubbles and bloating for both Wes and I.

Oh no! Have I turned into
"one of those people?"

Blogger alert!

It had to start with research. It had to be something I believed to be true. It had to make sense to me. I had jumped on so many band wagons in the past and fell right off the other side because I didn't really believe in the concept. I like meat, we have already established this, right? So, what meats are better for me? Does it depend on my blood type? WHAT? Blood type? Seriously, I have researched my blood type and have incorporated things I learned into my lifestyle.

Incorporating essential oils has been advancement in my research and belief system. No, I am not concocting love potions in my kitchen. Instead, I am using them in my cooking and incorporating them when I feel the thunder clouds roll in after cheating on purpose. Again, I am trying to give my body what it needs to right itself. I didn't want to make all of those healthy changes to turn around and put medication into my body. Oh dear, that may have come out wrong. I am not holistically treating an illness. I am simply incorporating a little Eastern medicine into my daily life.

We were watching television the other night. It was live, so we couldn't fast-forward through the commercials. The one that caught my attention was an ad for a new prescription medication for constipation and irritable bowel syndrome. The narrator went on and on about bloating and discomfort. So much, that by the end of the commercial, I looked over at Wes and shook my head.

"Why don't they figure out what the root cause is?"

"What?" he asked, looking up from his iPad.

"Watch this," I said. I rewound the commercial and we watched it together.

"I mean, did you hear the side effects? Blood in your stool, painful stomach cramps and diarrhea? Why don't the doctors look for the root cause rather than prescribing something that will just mask the symptoms?"

"Really?" Wes asked. "Babe, the prescription drug companies don't pay doctors to find the root cause. They pay doctors to prescribe their medication." He huffed, like I was a complete moron.

I am not a complete moron, and yes what Wes said made total sense. I used to be constipated all of the time. (Sorry, too much information?) If I would have seen that commercial I might have even spoken to my doctor about it. It just makes me wonder why the prescription drug companies are running ads on television if for nothing more than to make all of us buy into their claim.

What if I told you that you could recalibrate your digestive system naturally by incorporating whole foods and essential oils? What if I told you that I am not longer having issues with my tummy? It is possible to feed your body what it needs in order to do what it was originally designed for.

I am going to leave you with some food for thought:

You have the following two choices.

1. Take this medication, but you will also need an addition prescription to counteract the side-effects. Eventually, you will find that the medication doesn't work and another magical pill will appear on the market.

2. Find the root cause and treat it. (Pickled foods are a natural way to bring balance to your digestive track. I eat sour kraut quite often to keep things moving in the right direction.)

Have I piqued your interest, but you still want to know more? Okay, as I said before...you have to believe in something before you commit to changing your entire world. I could continue to share what I have learned, but honestly this book would never end. I am learning new things every single day. Each time I power up my laptop or prepare a new recipe I find something to add to this book.

I started a blog and a Facebook group for you and me to share the rest of our journey together. I wish I had the magic answer for you. I do. If I knew exactly what you needed to lose the fat suit, I promise I would give it to you in a heartbeat. I don't. I'm sorry. I can share everything I have learned, but I don't know everything. Man, if I did…I would totally write *that* book!

The links are in the back of the book, but I will place them here for convenience.

Blog:
http://livingcleanandhealthy.blogspot.com

Facebook page:
https://www.facebook.com/groups/NottaDiet

Come and join me!

Don't throw in the towel quite yet.

Who's the Girl in the **Fat Suit**?

She's every woman who has ever stood in front of a full-length mirror and asked, "Really?"

She's the woman standing next to you in line in the grocery store hoping silently no one mistakes her for a pregnant person.

She is the woman staring at thirty-seven mascara tubes reading the labels carefully, and wondering if fake eyelashes are the solution to distract from the ever-plumping Fat Suit.

She is the woman wearing the over-sized sweatshirt around the house. The reason she does this is to give her "suck-it-in" muscles a short break.

She is the woman behind the keyboard ordering clothes online in the safety of her own home. She is also the woman surely disappointed by twenty-something salesclerks with perky *everythings*.

She is the woman wearing body shaping clothes trying to conceal the discomfort, if only for a few hours.

She's a sugar fiend, a juicer, a meat-eater and willing to try just about anything other than swallowing a tape worm to lose weight.

She is the woman none of us expected to become, but find ourselves face-to-face with each morning. (Hopefully, the bathroom mirror is fogged.)

She is the woman searching for a solution for self-esteem, weight loss and happiness.

The girl in the Fat Suit is so much larger than me. (No pun intended, I promise.) It truly is many, many women I know and many women I have never met.

If you are like me, and find that you need a change...a healthier change...it is possible! You can take control over your weight, your mental health and you will find the tools to do so! Trust me, it is possible.

On December 23, 2013, I weighed two-hundred, twenty-nine pounds. As of April 5, 2014, I weigh one-hundred, seventy-six pounds! I have found and I am whole-heartedly committed to a healthier lifestyle.

I was feeling so good that I have even begun adding in some exercise! (For me, this was huge.) I felt better inside and out.

I whole-heartedly believed this would be the inspiration I needed to kick the smoking habit. As soon as I can't workout efficiently because of my lack of lung capacity...what other choice would I have? (Fingers crossed, please.)

Never give up. Never. Keep positive, patient and give yourself more credit. Remember, you are harder on yourself than anyone else could ever be. If you dodge the mirror...make the commitment to change.

It is hard! Oh my gosh, is it ever! But, you are worth it. You deserve to look into the mirror and see a reflection that makes you smile rather than cringe.

Trust me—once you figure out what it is you want to become—the process has already started.

March 23, 2014
179 pounds

Oh, and for the record, I just want to say that I am wearing tighter shirts! I take back what I wrote earlier about women who wear tight shirts. Here's the thing—I have started to realize how much better I feel—and my judgment was skewed by my own self-issues. I was placing judgment on others based on my own insecurities.

So not fair! I get it now. I do. I understand what it is like to stand in front of the mirror and be proud of my progress. I understand how it feels to show off what has been accomplished.

I know there are still women, smaller than I, who may see me in public and cringe—as I use to. I am okay with that. I am not where I want to end up quite yet, but darn it, I am starting to see the damage I caused myself by placing opinions on others.

If you are happy, truly happy within your skin—should it matter what other people think? No! Absolutely not! I wish I would have written this book ten, even five years ago. I wish I would have started controlling my weight when I was twenty-something. I wish I would have been able to accept myself at a size sixteen.

Oh, but the reality is, I wasn't ready. I wasn't ready to confront my own demons until today. I wasn't ready to look at the woman in the mirror and recognize the potential she had.

It took me ten years and one-hundred, seventeen pounds of additional weight, this book and support from my family, friends and Wes to finally make a commitment to myself. I hope to see you on Facebook and my blog. I can see us swapping stories and helping eachother in ways I can't even imagine right now. Until then, I send you my sincerest appreciate for sharing the journey so far.

Chin up! Shoulders back! You can do whatever you set your mind to.

Recipes

Recipe: Spaghetti Sauce
(Makes 8 servings)

8-10	Roma tomatoes chopped
6-8	On the vine tomatoes chopped
7	Cloves garlic peeled
½	Purple or Walla Walla onions chopped
¼ c.	Dried basil
¼ c.	Dried rosemary
2 T.	Dried oregano
¼ c.	Balsamic vinegar
1 T.	Olive oil
16 oz.	Tomato paste

Add balsamic vinegar and oil to blender. Add tomatoes, onions and garlic. Puree mixture and place into crockpot* or large sauce pan.*
Add basil, rosemary and oregano to sauce. Stir in the tomato paste. Cover and cook for 3-4 hours.

*Crockpot setting low, stovetop setting low.

(See Meatball recipe on next page.)

Recipe: Meatballs
(Makes 8 servings)

1 lb.	Grass-fed beef burger
1 lb.	Organic pork sausage
2 T.	Garlic powder
2 T.	Minced onion
1	Egg
½ c.	Bread crumbs (wheat)
¼ c.	Warm water

Mix all ingredients in a large bowl. Roll into meatballs the size of golf balls and add to sauce. (Don't pre-cook your meatballs.)
Allow meatballs to cook in the sauce for 3-4 hours.

Recipe: Orange Glazed Salmon
(Makes 4 servings)

4	Salmon fillets
¼ c.	Honey
2	Large oranges, juiced
½ c.	Water
1 T.	Flax seeds (set aside)

Mix dark brown sugar, juice and water in a bowl. Choose a method from below. Pour mixture over Salmon and cook. Sprinkle with Flax Seeds and serve with a salad.

Oven at 350° for 20 minutes covered.

BBQ in aluminum foil med heat for 15 minutes.

Sauce pan over medium heat for 15-20 minutes. (Covered)

Recipe: Tropical Juice
(Makes 2 servings)

4	Large oranges
1	Lemon
1	Pineapple
20	Carrots
1"	Ginger root
½	Cucumber

Follow your juicers recommendations and juice the above.

Place liquid in blender and add:

3	Bananas
1	Avocado

Blend until smooth. Add ice or refrigerate until cold. (This is one of my favorites! It is thick and creamy and oh so good.)

Recipe: Morning Juice
(Makes 2 servings)

4	Oranges
6	Golden Delicious apples
2	Pears
1	Cucumber
¼"	Ginger root
10-12	Carrots
1	Lemon

Prepare the fruit according to your juicer recommendations. (If I am making cookies out of the pulp, I will remove the core and stems from the apples and pears.)

Juice and add ice. For an added boost, place the juice in blender and add a banana. For an afternoon boost, replace banana with half an avocado. Creamy goodness, if you can get past the color!

Recipe: Juice Pulp Cookies
(Makes 2 dozen)

1 c.	Juice pulp
½ c.	Organic peanut or almond butter
2	Eggs
1 T.	Vanilla
2 tsp.	Baking soda
¼ c.	Dark chocolate chips
1 c.	Old fashioned oats
2 c.	Wheat flour

**Optional: Dried cranberries, almond slivers, coconut or raisins.

Combine juice pulp, peanut or almond butter, vanilla and eggs in mixer until smooth. Add dry ingredients until mixed.

Preheat oven to 350°

Drop rounded teaspoons onto baking sheets. Bake 8-10 minutes until golden brown. Smash gently with spatula and let cool.

Recipe: Crockpot Chicken
(Makes 4 servings)

4	Chicken breasts
¼ c.	Balsamic vinegar
1"	Ginger root peeled and minced
1	Large Onion diced
5	Garlic cloves minced
½ c.	Water

Combine all ingredients (except chicken) and pour into crockpot. Place chicken in crockpot and cook on low for 3-8 hours until chicken shreds easily with a fork.

Serve with a salad or jasmine rice.

Recipe: Easy, delicious veggies
(Makes 4 servings)

1 pc.	Bacon chopped*
1 c.	Broccoli (bite size)
1 c.	Cauliflower (bite size)
1 c.	Carrots diced
1	Handful green beans or asparagus
¼ c.	Chopped cilantro (set aside)

In a medium sauté pan, begin layering ingredients beginning with the bacon. Cover and sauté on medium for 10 minutes.

Plate and top with chopped cilantro.

Recipe: BBQ Sauce

10	Roma tomatoes diced
6	On the vine tomatoes diced
1	Bell pepper (red or yellow) diced
½ c.	Apple cider vinegar
1 c.	Brown sugar
2 t.	Garlic Powder
1 t.	Onion powder
1 T.	Crushed pepper flakes for heat (optional)

Combine tomatoes, peppers and vinegar in blender until smooth. (Puree setting works the best.)

Pour into sauce pan on medium heat and add brown sugar and spices. Cook on medium heat, stirring constantly until brown sugar is dissolved.

Refrigerate in an airtight container. Use within 60 days.

Recipe: Easy Salad Dressing

1 c.	Olive oil
1 c.	Red wine vinegar
2 ½ tsp.	each garlic powder, dried oregano, and basil
2 tsp.	Pepper
2 tsp.	Onion powder
2 tsp.	Dijon Mustard
5	Kalamata olives (pitted)

Combine all ingredients in blender until smooth.

Refrigerate in an airtight container and use within 1 month.

**Great as a chicken or pork marinade as well as a fresh salad dressing.

Recipe: Baked Oysters
(Makes 4 servings)

12	Large oysters, cleaned and shucked
1 c.	Coconut or Almond milk

Add oysters to milk and set aside.

Mix the following ingredients in a large bowl:

3 c.	Wheat flour
1 T.	Dried dill
1 T.	Garlic powder
1 T.	Onion powder
1 T.	Pepper

Place cookie cooling racks on baking sheets.
(This will allow the breading to cook and become
crunchy even on the underside.)

Preheat oven to 375°

Double dredge the oysters in milk then dry
followed by milk then dried again.
Bake 15 minutes.
For additional crunch, broil and addition 3-4
minutes. (Keep an eye on them! This will happen
quickly.)

Serve with Tartar Sauce (next page)

Recipe: Tatar Sauce

1	White onion chopped fine
4 c.	Greek yogurt
1 T.	Dried dill
1	Juiced lemon
½ tsp.	White pepper (black is also ok)

Combine all ingredients. Refrigerate in an airtight container overnight.

Use within 2 weeks.

Gratitude

I have so much to be thankful for. If I tried to thank every single person who has had a profound effect on my life, it would seriously be a ga-zillion pages. Honestly, I think you would probably get bored and close the book before you ever read my amazingly inspired biography. (Ok, it really isn't all that amazing or inspired. Do you know how hard it is to write about yourself in third person? It's like trying to convince everyone that you are some faultless writer. I am faulted, as you now know.)

Here's a quick little run down of people I have either admired for their ability to carry their weight without regret, helped me discover who I am, or those people I have simply driven to eat sugar to keep up with my antics.

They are not in any order: My parents, brothers, grandparents, in-laws...oh dear, we are starting to get too many. Okay, I will limit this small paragraph to my family either by blood marriage or other circumstances. I love each of you dearly and appreciate your support.

I must say though, my husband, Wes deserves his own paragraph. I mean, look at what he has to put up with. I am obviously not the easiest woman to be married to. I am thankful for his patience and his unwavering love of me at any size. He is honestly the only living person who knows my every single insecurity I have and he still loves me. (I am a very lucky girl, I know.)

I am grateful for Gwen Lindsey, and her ability to design an amazing book cover. I tried to convey my feelings of standing on front of the mirror looking at a larger than life portrait of myself. Gwen ran with it and I must say she nailed it!

To Frozen Ladybug for reading and catching all of my silly errors. Oh, and the not so silly errors too. She suggested numerous re-writes and read so many drafts! I swear, she probably has the entire book memorized by now. This book would not be what it is without her.

To Meghan Hyde at Hyde-n-Seek Editing, for enhancing my voice. I appreciate her talents along with her supportive comments and emails. She helped my organize the flow and encouraged me to include chapters I had originally expressed hesitation on. This book may have been much shorter if it hadn't been for her input and patience.

To my friends who have supported me, and stood wide-eyed while I shared some of the chapters in this book. Yes, I really weighed two-hundred, twenty-nine pounds. I know many of you still don't believe that fact, so I thought by putting it out there for everyone to see may convince the inconvincible.

To all of my fans! I love each of you dearly and hope you know just how much you have helped me, whether it was during a writer's block, or a rant about size four sales clerks! Thank you for fanning me.

Special thanks to Steven and Izabelle with Eight Paws Publishing, LLC. I must admit, naming a publishing company after two mischievous canines was a special task for those involved.

And last, but certainly not least, thank you for purchasing this book over all of the many on the market. I sincerely hope you enjoyed it and found my sense of humor somewhat funny. I hope you found my journey somewhat inspiring. You can lose the Fat Suit if you decide living within it just causes you grief.

About the Author

A. L. Elder grew up in Idaho Falls, Idaho where she spent most of her childhood riding her horse and following her grandfather from the garden to the pasture.

She has lived in Idaho, Montana, Utah, Hawaii and Oregon. She now calls the Willamette Valley her home and never wishes to pack or unpack another moving box again. She shares a beautiful farm house with her husband, Wes and yellow Labrador, Steve.

Her love for storytelling began at an early age when her father presented her with an old fashioned typewriter. Her first writing was a play about the infamous Knights of the Round Table at age nine.

Adulthood responsibilities took the place of writing until 2012 when she enrolled in college and took a creative writing class. Soon after, she picked up a fountain pen and began scribbling an idea for a memoir.

Hey Lady … are these your underwear? was published in 2013 and the dam restraining her creativity, broke. A flood of ideas replaced the once absent need to write.

Obsessed with the new adventure, Wes decided to build a room dedicated to her passion

for writing.

When A. L. Elder is not at work, attending college classes, or taking on adventures with her family, you can find her in her office typing away on a comical and heartfelt rendition of her crazy life.

Contact information

Feel free to follow her via,
Twitter: @alelderauthor #nottadiet
Facebook: AuthorALELder
https://www.facebook.com/groups/Notta
Diet/
Email: a.l.elder2012@gmail

Other offerings from April...

Hey Lady...

A book filled with mostly true stories from the life of A. L. Elder. This book takes the reader on a journey through childhood adventures, tenacious-teenage-tasks and adulthood mishaps. A comical look back at the moments in life when lessons were learned and crying was not an option.

April survived the interrogation process of her parents, learned that gilding and a gelding were two different things and became a stalker to win the heart of her future husband.

Somewhere along the way, her skirt got tucked into her tights and her dog ate her underwear.

Available now on kindle, in paperback—normal and large font—where your favorite books are sold.

Coming Soon!

One D.I.Y. from DIVORCE

When Wes and I decided to move back to Oregon, there were a few things about his childhood home that needed some love. What we didn't realize is that we would eventually remodel the entire house. Together!

If you have ever done a do-it-yourself project, you know the trouble that can happen. This book will be filled with trouble, arguments, decorating drama and moments when we both stared at piles of carpet wondering what we were doing.

At one point, Wes and I looked at eachother and agreed that we were one D.I.Y. project from divorce. (Of course, that wasn't true...we did three more rooms after that!)

Made in the USA
Lexington, KY
02 January 2016